CONGRESSIONAL POLICIES, PRACTICES AND PROCEDURES

CONGRESSIONAL GOLD MEDALS

1776-2013

CONGRESSIONAL POLICIES, PRACTICES AND PROCEDURES

Additional books in this series can be found on Nova's website under the Series tab.

Additional E-books in this series can be found on Nova's website under the E-book tab.

CONGRESSIONAL POLICIES, PRACTICES AND PROCEDURES

CONGRESSIONAL GOLD MEDALS

1776-2013

AMANDA PERRY-JENKINS
EDITOR

NOVINKA

New York

Library of Congress Cataloging-in-Publication Data

ISBN: 978-1-62948-848-6

Published by Nova Science Publishers, Inc. † New York

CONTENTS

PREFACE

This book responds to congressional inquiries concerning the nature, history, and contemporary application of the process for awarding Gold Medals, and includes a historical examination and chronological list of these awards.

Chapter 1 – Senators and Representatives are frequently asked to support or sponsor proposals recognizing historic events and outstanding achievements by individuals or institutions. Among the various forms of recognition that Congress bcstows, the Congressional Gold Medal is often considered the most distinguished. Through this venerable tradition, the occasional commissioning of individually struck gold medals in its name, Congress has expressed public gratitude on behalf of the nation for distinguished contributions for more than two centuries. Since 1776, this award, which initially was bestowed on military leaders, has also been given to such diverse individuals as Sir Winston Churchill and Bob Hope, George Washington and Robert Frost, Joe Louis and Mother Teresa of Calcutta. Most recently, a Congressional Gold Medal was awarded to Raoul Wallenberg in recognition of his achievements and heroic actions during the Holocaust.

Members of Congress and their staff frequently ask questions concerning the nature, history, and contemporary application of the process for awarding Gold Medals. This report responds to congressional inquiries concerning this process, and includes a historical examination and chronological list of these awards. It is intended to assist Members of Congress and staff in their consideration of future Gold Medal proposals, and will be updated as Gold Medals are approved.

George Washington, Bob Hope, Joe Louis, the Wright Brothers, Robert Frost, Francis Albert "Frank" Sinatra, and Mother Teresa of Calcutta share a common bond in American history. These notable personages, together with approximately 300 other individuals and the American Red Cross, have been accorded the unique distinction of being awarded a Congressional Gold Medal. Through these awards, Congress has expressed public gratitude for distinguished contributions, dramatized the virtues of patriotism, and perpetuated the remembrance of great events. This tradition, of authorizing individually struck gold medals bearing the portraits of those so honored or images of events in which they participated, is rich with history.

Although Congress has approved legislation stipulating specific requirements for numerous other awards and decorations,[1] there are no permanent statutory provisions specifically relating to the creation of Congressional Gold Medals. When such an award has been deemed appropriate, Congress has, by special action, provided for the creation of a personalized medal to be given in its name, which would in each instance truly record the approbation of a grateful country.

Chapter 2 – This is the Public Law 113-11 (Congressional Gold Medal posthumously awarded to Addie Mae Collins, Denise McNair, Carole Robertson, and Cynthia Wesley).

Chapter 3 – This is the Public Law 113-16 (Congressional Gold Medal, collectively, to the First Special Service Force, World War II).

In: Congressional Gold Medals: 1776-2013 ISBN: 978-1-62948-848-6
Editor: Amanda Perry-Jenkins

Chapter 1

CONGRESSIONAL GOLD MEDALS, 1776-2012*

Matthew Eric Glassman

SUMMARY

Senators and Representatives are frequently asked to support or sponsor proposals recognizing historic events and outstanding achievements by individuals or institutions. Among the various forms of recognition that Congress bestows, the Congressional Gold Medal is often considered the most distinguished. Through this venerable tradition, the occasional commissioning of individually struck gold medals in its name, Congress has expressed public gratitude on behalf of the nation for distinguished contributions for more than two centuries. Since 1776, this award, which initially was bestowed on military leaders, has also been given to such diverse individuals as Sir Winston Churchill and Bob Hope, George Washington and Robert Frost, Joe Louis and Mother Teresa of Calcutta. Most recently, a Congressional Gold Medal was awarded to Raoul Wallenberg in recognition of his achievements and heroic actions during the Holocaust.

Members of Congress and their staff frequently ask questions concerning the nature, history, and contemporary application of the process for awarding Gold Medals. This report responds to congressional inquiries concerning this

---

* This is an edited, reformatted and augmented version of the Congressional Research Service Publication, CRS Report for Congress RL30076, dated May 30, 2013.

process, and includes a historical examination and chronological list of these awards. It is intended to assist Members of Congress and staff in their consideration of future Gold Medal proposals, and will be updated as Gold Medals are approved.

George Washington, Bob Hope, Joe Louis, the Wright Brothers, Robert Frost, Francis Albert "Frank" Sinatra, and Mother Teresa of Calcutta share a common bond in American history. These notable personages, together with approximately 300 other individuals and the American Red Cross, have been accorded the unique distinction of being awarded a Congressional Gold Medal. Through these awards, Congress has expressed public gratitude for distinguished contributions, dramatized the virtues of patriotism, and perpetuated the remembrance of great events. This tradition, of authorizing individually struck gold medals bearing the portraits of those so honored or images of events in which they participated, is rich with history.

Although Congress has approved legislation stipulating specific requirements for numerous other awards and decorations,[1] there are no permanent statutory provisions specifically relating to the creation of Congressional Gold Medals. When such an award has been deemed appropriate, Congress has, by special action, provided for the creation of a personalized medal to be given in its name, which would in each instance truly record the approbation of a grateful country.

PRACTICES ADOPTED DURING THE AMERICAN REVOLUTION

Congress from the outset was "imbued with the conviction that only the very highest achievements [were] entitled to such a distinction, and that the value of a reward is enhanced by its rarity!"[2] Instituting such a tradition was considered "both a legitimate function and powerful instrument of nationality."[3] "Few inventions," Colonel David Humphrey wrote in 1787, "could be more happily calculated to diffuse the knowledge and preserve the memory of illustrious characters and splendid events than medals—whether we take into consideration the imperishable nature of the substance whence they are formed, the facility of multiplying copies, or the practice of depositing them in the cabinets of the curious."[4] With these words, Humphrey, who had the responsibility for having the first gold medals struck in Paris, captured the essence of the feelings which inspired the Continental Congress to choose medals as its highest distinction and expression of national appreciation.[5]

Following a long-standing historical practice, Congress commissioned gold medals as tributes for what were considered to be the most distinguished achievements. Silver and bronze medals, and ceremonial swords, were awarded for less eminent, but still notable, accomplishments.[6] Of these, only the gold medal has been continuously awarded to the present day.

The Continental Congress had not yet proclaimed its independence from Great Britain when, on March 25, 1776, George Washington, commander of the Continental Army, was tendered the first Congressional Gold Medal for his "wise and spirited conduct" in bringing about British evacuation of Boston.[7] During the next 12 years, the Continental Congress authorized an additional six gold medals for Revolutionary military and naval leaders.

In 1777, Major General Horatio Gates was recognized for his "brave and successful efforts" in bringing about the surrender of the British Army at Saratoga. Two years later, a similar honor was bestowed upon Major General Anthony Wayne in 1779 for his courageous assault on the British at Stony Point, NY.[8]

A gold medal was also given to Major Henry Lee in commemoration of the skill and bravery he exhibited against the British at Paulus Hook, NJ. Brigadier General Daniel Morgan and Major General Nathaniel Greene were praised for their gallant efforts in South Carolina during 1781. Six years later, John Paul Jones was similarly honored for his "valor and brilliant services" in capturing the *Serapis.*[9]

First Medals Were Struck in Paris

While the Continental Congress was prompt in approving each of these medals, those responsible for carrying out the wishes of Congress were far less expeditious. Because of its close ties with France, Congress turned to Paris for advice and assistance in having the medals struck. Unfortunately, Congress's preoccupation with the American Revolution, together with the lengthy and complicated procedures which had to be followed in Paris, produced long delays.

Thomas Jefferson was not able to present Washington his gold medal until March 21, 1790, some 14 years after it had been approved. At the same time, Washington received a mahogany box containing a number of other gold medals ordered by Congress. Soon thereafter, these medals were transmitted by the former President to the various recipients.[10] The gold medal conferred upon Major Henry "Light Horse Harry" Lee for his "remarkable prudence" and "bravery" during the surprise raid of Paulus Hook, NJ, was the first to be struck in this country.[11]

RECIPIENTS IN THE NINETEENTH CENTURY

Following the ratification of the Constitution, the first gold medal authorized by the Congress of the United States was given to Captain Thomas Truxtun in 1800 for his gallant effort during the action between the United States frigate *Constellation* and the French ship *La Vengeance*. In 1805, Commodore Edward Preble received a gold medal for gallantry and good conduct during the War with Tripoli.[12]

War of 1812

Subsequently, Congress commissioned 27 gold medals for notable victories and achievements in the War of 1812. This was more than four times as many as it had given during the American Revolution. "Scarcely a victory of any consequence was overlooked."[13] The gold medal Congress approved on February 22, 1816, honoring Captain James Biddle's "gallantry" in capturing the British sloop-of-war *Penguin* was the final naval award of this character awarded by Congress until World War II.[14]

Mexican War

Gold medals would continue to be awarded for military achievements until the Civil War, but with far less frequency. In part this is explained by the fact that in the War with Mexico naval operations were negligible and military operations were principally confined to two expeditions led, respectively, by Major General Zachary Taylor and Major General Winfield Scott.

Taylor's heroics against the Mexicans earned him gold medals on three different occasions.[15] Scott, for his efforts, was accorded a gold medal in 1848.[16] Gold medals were also given to 10 officers and seamen belonging or attached to the French, British, and Spanish ships-of-war, who on December

10, 1846, gallantly rescued 37 of the officers and crew from the wreck of the United States brig *Somers* in Vera Cruz harbor.[17]

Heroic action of a very different type in 1854 prompted Congress to praise Commander Duncan N. Ingraham of the U.S.S. *St. Louis* for his efforts in rescuing Martin Koszta from illegal seizure and imprisonment aboard the Austrian war-brig *Hussar*.[18]

Congress Broadens the Scope of Its Gold Medal

Soon after the *Hussar* episode, Congress broke with its tradition of only honoring heroism associated with the actions of American military or naval personnel. In 1858, Dr. Frederick A. Rose, an assistant-surgeon in the British Navy, was recognized for his kindness and humanity to sick American seamen aboard the U.S. steamer *Susquehannah* whose crew had been stricken with yellow fever.[19] At the behest of President Abraham Lincoln, Congress applauded Cornelius Vanderbilt in 1864 for his patriotic gift to the imperiled nation of a steamship which bore the donor's name.[20] Three years later, Cyrus W. Field was praised for his work in the laying of the transatlantic cable.[21] Tribute was similarly paid to Private George F. Robinson for his "heroic conduct" in saving Secretary of State William H. Seward from an assassin's knife on April 14, 1865.[22]

At the same time, Congress established the first permanent American military decoration with creation of the Medal of Honor. This award, which was conceived in the early 1860s, marked the beginning of a formalized policy by the United States of awarding military decorations. Although this medal was also to be presented in the name of the Congress of the United States and today is often referred to as the Congressional Medal of Honor, the regulations for awarding the Medal of Honor have from the beginning been the responsibility of the armed services.[23] There is a clear distinction between the Medal of Honor, which is a military award, and Congressional Gold Medals, which are authorized by Congress to honor particular individuals and events.

During the Civil War, more than 1,500 Americans were awarded the Medal of Honor, but only one individual—Ulysses S. Grant—received a Congressional Gold Medal.[24] Thirty-five years were to pass before Congress would bestow the award on another American military leader.

On five occasions, in the interim, Congress expressed its gratitude for lifesaving contributions. In 1866 three merchant sea captains were recognized with gold medals for rescuing some 500 men from the wreck of the steamship

San Francisco more than a decade earlier. In 1873, Congress expressed its admiration for the 10 men from Westerly, RI, who saved the lives of 32 persons from the wrecked steamer *Metis*, in the waters of Long Island Sound.[25]

The following year, the heroics of John Horn, Jr., who during an 11-year period had rescued 110 men, women, and children from drowning in the Detroit River, captured the attention of Congress.[26] Joseph Francis was thanked in 1888 for his "life-long service to humanity" in the construction and perfection of lifesaving appliances, which had been instrumental in saving several hundreds of lives.[27] In 1890, George Wallace Melville, chief engineer aboard the Arctic exploring steamer *Jeannette*, and seven of his shipmates were praised for their persistent efforts to find and assist their commanding officer after they became shipwrecked.[28]

Nineteenth-century contributions of a far different nature prompted expressions of gratitude to philanthropists George Peabody of Massachusetts and John F. Slater of Connecticut for their substantial financial support for education of the underprivileged in the South and Southwest.[29]

RECIPIENTS IN THE 20TH AND 21ST CENTURIES

In the 20th and 21st centuries, Congress continued to broaden the scope of such honors to include recognition of excellence in such varied fields as the arts, athletics, aviation, diplomacy, entertainment, exploration, medicine, politics, religion, and science.

Actors, Artists, Authors, Entertainers, and Musicians

Nineteen Americans from the arts and the world of entertainment have received Congressional Gold Medals to date. Composer George M. Cohan was the first to be so acclaimed, in 1936, for his patriotic songs "Over There" and "A Grand Old Flag." Some 18 years later, in recognition of Irving Berlin's brilliance in composing "God Bless America" and other patriotic songs, Congress bestowed its second gold medal on an American song writer.[30]

During the 1960s, poet Robert Frost was praised for enriching the culture of the world, comedian Bob Hope was honored for outstanding "service to his country and the cause of peace," and filmmaker Walt Disney was singled out for his "outstanding contributions to the United States and the world."[31] Opera singer and humanitarian Marian Anderson and actor John Wayne were similarly decorated for their distinguished careers and contributions to the nation and world in the late 1970s.[32]

Since 1980, author Louis L'Amour, choral music conductor Fred Waring; entertainer and humanitarian Danny Thomas; and author Elie Wiesel, one of the foremost spokesmen of the victims of the Holocaust, were so honored.[33] Singer Harry Chapin was recognized for his efforts to address issues of hunger around the world.[34] In addition, Congress has memorialized the contributions of George and Ira Gershwin to American music, theater, and culture; Aaron Copland to American music composition; Andrew Wyeth to American art; Frank Sinatra to the entertainment industry through his endeavors as a producer, director, actor, and vocalist; and Charles M. Schulz to comic illustration.[35] In 2008, Constantino Brumidi was recognized for his contributions to the nation as a designer and decorator of the U.S. Capitol.[36]

Aeronautical and Space Pioneers

Gold medals for outstanding contributions in air and space exploration have covered a broad spectrum of accomplishments. In a public ceremony at Dayton, Ohio, on June 18, 1909, Wilbur and Orville Wright were presented Congressional Gold Medals for their achievements in demonstrating to the world the potential of aerial navigation.[37]

Congress recognized Charles A. Lindbergh for his aeronautical achievements in 1928.[38] A year later, the seven officers and men who conceived, organized, and commanded the first trans- Atlantic flight in the United States naval flying boat NC-4 were honored. Howard Hughes was praised in 1939 for "advancing the science of aviation." At the close of World War II, Congress authorized a gold medal for American military aviation pioneer Brigadier General William (Billy) Mitchell.[39]

In September 1959, Dr. Robert H. Goddard's "historic pioneering research on space rockets, missiles, and jet propulsion" was acclaimed by Congress. Since that time, gold medals have been given to Lieutenant General Ira C. Eaker for his "distinguished career as an aviation pioneer and Air Force leader"; and to the first transatlantic balloonists: Ben Abruzzo, Maxie Anderson, and Larry Newman.[40]

Four decades later, in conjunction with the 40th anniversary of mankind's historic and first lunar landing in 1969, Congress honored Neil A. Armstrong, the first human to walk on the Moon; Edwin E. "Buzz" Aldrin, Jr., the pilot of the lunar module and second person to walk on the Moon; Michael Collins, the pilot of their Apollo 11 mission's command module; and John Herschel Glenn, Jr., who, in 1962, became the first American to orbit the Earth.[41]

Antarctic Explorers

Congressional tributes have also been extended to several explorers of Antarctica. American explorer Lincoln Ellsworth received a gold medal for his polar flight of 1925 and transpolar flight of 1926. Also participating in the latter flight, and similarly honored, were Norwegian explorer Roald Amundsen and Italian explorer Umberto Nobile.[42]

The undaunted services rendered by Rear Admiral Richard E. Byrd and the other members of the Byrd Expedition were praised with equal exuberance in 1930. Six years later, Lincoln Ellsworth received a second gold medal for his claims on behalf of the United States of approximately 350,000 square miles in Antarctica and for his 2,500-mile aerial survey of the heart of Antarctica.[43]

Acclaimed Lifesavers

Despite the fact that several different lifesaving medals have been provided for over the years by law,[44] Congress has still periodically expressed its own admiration for acts of heroism. In 1865, Congress praised George F. Robinson for his heroic conduct in fighting off an assassin attempting to kill Secretary of State William H. Seward.[45] Two American sea captains, Captain Edwin J. Low, of the bark *Kilby* of Boston, and Captain George C. Stouffer, of the ship *Antarctic* of New York, were recognized in 1866 for aiding in the rescue of some 500 men from the wreck of the steamship *San Francisco*.[46] Six years later, Congress lauded Captain Jared S. Crandall and nine other men of Westerly, RI, for manning a life-boat and a fishing boat to save the lives of 32 persons from the wreck of the steamer *Metis* on the waters of Long Island Sound.[47] A Gold Medal was awarded to John Horn, Jr., in 1874 for his heroic exploits in rescuing 110 men, women, and children from drowning in Detroit River.[48] Congress in 1888 acknowledged the work of Joseph Francis in the construction and perfection of life-saving appliances by which many thousands of lives have been saved.[49]

In 1902, three members of the Revenue Cutter Service were praised for a nearly 2,000-mile overland relief expedition to the American whaling fleet in the arctic region. At a March 1, 1913, White House ceremony, Captain Arthur Henry Rostron, commander of the steamship *Carpathia*, received a gold medal from President William Howard Taft for his prompt and heroic response in rescuing 704 survivors from the wreck of the *Titanic*. The following March, Captain Paul H. Kreibohm of the American steamer *Kroonland*, and four members of his crew, were awarded gold medals for rescuing 89 people from the burning steamer *Volturno* in the North Atlantic.[50]

Rev. Francis X. Quinn, pastor of the Church of the Guardian Angel in New York City, was honored in 1939 for risking his life in persuading an armed gunman holding an elderly couple hostage to surrender to police. The following January, a medal was authorized for William Sinnott, who had been wounded while guarding Franklin D. Roosevelt in Miami just prior to his first inauguration. A year later, 11-year-old Roland Boucher of Burlington, VT, saved the lives of four children who had broken through the ice on Lake Champlain near Juniper Island. Congress saluted Boucher's bravery and heroism in 1943.[51]

Distinguished Military Personnel

In 1900, Congress once again returned to the practice of recognizing distinguished military service when it praised First Lieutenant Frank H. Newcomb, commander of the revenue cutter *Hudson* for rescuing the United States naval torpedo boat *Winslow* under a "most galling fire from the enemy's guns."[52] At the conclusion of World War II, the valor, bravery, and heroism of Fleet Admiral Ernest J. King and General of the Army George C. Marshall, two of America's most able military leaders during the war, were recognized. Also in 1946, General John J. Pershing was honored for his "heroic achievements" as Commander in Chief of the American Expeditionary Forces in Europe in World War I and for his "unselfish devotion to the service of his country" during World War II.[53] The four known surviving veterans of the Civil War received Congressional Gold Medals a decade later.[54]

Rear Admiral Hyman George Rickover was applauded in 1958 for his achievements in "directing the development and construction of the world's first nuclear-powered ships and the first large- scale nuclear power reactor devoted exclusively to the production of electricity." A quarter of a century later, Rickover was accorded a second gold medal for his contributions to the "development of safe nuclear energy and the defense of the United States."[55] Meanwhile, in 1962, Congress authorized a Congressional Gold Medal for

General Douglas MacArthur in recognition of his "gallant service" to the United States.[56]

Three other military leaders were so acclaimed in the 1990s. General Matthew B. Ridgeway's more than 40 years of distinguished service as a military commander earned recognition at the beginning of the decade. Following Operation Desert Storm, which culminated with the successful liberation of the nation of Kuwait, General H. Norman Schwarzkopf and General Colin L. Powell were honored. Schwarzkopf was cited for his "exemplary performance as a military leader in coordinating the planning, strategy, and execution of the United States" and coalition forces in liberating Kuwait. Powell was recognized for his "exemplary performance as a military leader and advisor to the President in planning and coordinating the military response to the Iraqi invasion of Kuwait."[57]

In 2000, Congress recognized the contribution of the original 29 Navajo Marine Corps Radio Operators, known as the "Navajo Code Talkers," who developed a code using their native language to communicate military messages during World War II. The code developed by these Native Americans proved to be unbreakable and was used extensively throughout the Pacific theater. Military commanders credited use of the Navajo Code with "saving lives of countless American soldiers and the success of the engagements of Guadalcanal, Tarawa, Saipan, Iwo Jima, and Okinawa."[58] With the Code Talkers Recognition Act of 2008, Congress recognized the dedication and valor of Native American code talkers from other tribes for their contributions to United States victories in World War I and World War II.[59]

General Henry H. Shelton, Chairman of the Joint Chiefs of Staff (October 1997-September 2001), was honored in 2001 for his leadership in coordinating the United States and NATO successful combat action throughout Operation Allied Force in the Balkans.[60]

In a unique action early in 2006, Congress honored the Tuskegee Airmen collectively with a single Congressional Gold Medal in recognition of their unique military record, which inspired revolutionary reform in the Armed Forces. The presentation ceremony was held in the Capitol Rotunda on Thursday, March 29, 2007. Following presentation by the President, the medal was given to the Smithsonian Institution, where it was to be displayed.[61] Congress used a similar approach in 2009, awarding the Women Airforce Service Pilots of World War II collectively for their "pioneering military service and exemplary record." The "'WASP," as they were known, were the first women in history to fly American military aircraft. This medal, like the

Tuskegee Gold Medal, is to be given to the Smithsonian Institution for display as appropriate.[62] In 2010, another collective medal was awarded, to the 110th Infantry Battalion and the 442nd Regimental Combat Team, United States Army, in recognition of their "bravery, valor, and dedication to country ... while fighting a 2-fronted battle of discrimination at home and fascism abroad."[63]

Two other collective medals were awarded in 2011. The first was awarded to the Montford Point Marines, in recognition of "their personal sacrifice and service to their country" as the first African-American Marines. [64] The second was awarded to all fallen heroes of 9/11, in "honor of the men and women who perished as a result of the terrorist attacks on the United States on September 11, 2001." [65]

Notables in Agriculture, Science, and Medicine

Historic achievements in agriculture, science, and medicine also have been watched closely by Congress. For discovering the cause and means of transmission of yellow fever, Major Walter Reed and his 21 associates were recognized in 1928. Gold medals were subsequently authorized for Mrs. Richard Aldrich and Anna Bouligny some four decades after their outstanding, unselfish, and wholly voluntary service in establishing and operating "hospitals for the care and treatment of military patients in Puerto Rico" during the War with Spain.[66]

Thomas A. Edison was honored for the development and application of "inventions that have revolutionized civilization." Similar congressional tributes were subsequently extended to Dr. Jonas E. Salk, for discovering a serum for the prevention of polio, to Dr. Thomas Anthony Dooley III for his unselfish medical care among the underprivileged peoples of the world, particularly in southeast Asia, and to Mary Lasker, whom some considered the first lady of medicine and science in this country, for her "humanitarian contributions in the area of medical research and education, urban beautification and the fine arts." Congress recognized Nobel Laureate Dr. Norman E. Borlaug, "whose accomplishments in terms of bringing radical change to world agriculture and uplifting humanity are without parallel." Internationally recognized physician and surgeon Dr. Michael Ellis DeBakey was lauded for his pioneering work in the field of cardiovascular surgery, as well as for his innovative research into this and other fields of medicine.[67]

Awards for Public Service, Athletic Prowess, Civil Rights Activism, and Humanitarian Contributions

The first politician to be honored with a gold medal was Vice President Alben W. Barkley in 1949.[68] Since that time, Congress has saluted the distinguished and dedicated public service of Sam Rayburn, Robert F. Kennedy, Hubert Humphrey, Harry S. Truman, former President Gerald R. Ford and his wife Betty, and former President Ronald Reagan and his wife Nancy. Tribute was also paid to Representative Leo J. Ryan, following his "untimely" assassination while performing his responsibilities as a Member of the House of Representatives in Guyana.[69] Most recently, former Senator Edward William Brooke III, of Massachusetts, the first African American elected by popular vote to the U.S. Senate, was recognized for his unprecedented and enduring service to our Nation.[70]

Athletes so recognized have been baseball hall of famers Roberto Clemente and Jackie Robinson, heavyweight boxing champion Joe Louis, track and field star Jesse Owens, and golfers Byron Nelson and Arnold Palmer. Clemente was also praised for his "civil, charitable, and humanitarian contributions," Robinson for "many contributions to the nation," Louis for bolstering the "spirit of American people during one of the most critical times in American history," Owens for his "humanitarian contributions to public service, civil rights, and international goodwill," Nelson "for his significant contributions ... as a teacher and a commentator, and Palmer for "his service to the Nation in promoting excellence and good sportsman in golf."[71]

A lifelong commitment to the principles of freedom, equality, justice, and peace earned civil rights worker Roy Wilkins acclaim on Capitol Hill. The Little Rock Nine—Jean Brown Trickey, Carlotta Walls LaNier, Melba Patillo Beals, Terrence Roberts, Gloria Ray Karlmark, Thelma Mothershed Wair, Ernest Green, Elizabeth Eckford, and Jefferson Thomas—were recognized for the selfless heroism they exhibited "in the cause of civil rights by integrating Central High School in Little Rock Arkansas." Rosa Parks, the "First Lady of Civil Rights," was honored for her "quiet dignity," which "ignited the most significant social movement in the history of the United States." Praise was bestowed on Dr. Dorothy Height for her contribution "as one of the preeminent social and civil rights activists of her time, particularly in the struggle for equality, social justice, and human rights for all people." Reverend Joseph A. DeLaine, Harry and Eliza Briggs, and Levi Pearson were saluted "for their contributions to the Nation as pioneers in the effort to desegregate public schools that led directly to the landmark desegregation case of Brown et al. v. the Board of Education of Topeka et al." Reverend Doctor Martin Luther King, Jr., and his wife Coretta Scott King, were lauded for their contribution "to the Nation on behalf of the civil rights movement." [72]

Sustained efforts to preserve the beauty of our nation prompted praise for Lady Bird Johnson and Laurence Spelman Rockefeller. Lady Bird was applauded for her "outstanding contributions to the improvement and beautification of America," and Rockefeller for his "leadership on behalf of natural resource conservation and historic preservation.[73]

Marking humanitarian efforts, twelve of the 53 gold medals awarded by the 103rd-106th Congresses were given to individuals who have dedicated their lives to the service of others. Rabbi Menachem Mendel Schneerson, the leader of the Lubavitch movement for more than four decades, was recognized for his "outstanding and enduring contributions toward world education, morality, and acts of charity." Billy Graham, "America's most respected and admired evangelical leader for the past half century," and his wife Ruth, were honored for "their outstanding and enduring contributions toward faith, morality, and charity."[74]

Former President Gerald Ford and his wife Betty were honored "their dedicated public service and outstanding humanitarian contributions to the people of the United States."[75]

Mother Teresa of Calcutta was acclaimed for her nearly 70 years of "selfless dedication to humanity and charitable works." Ecumenical Patrick Bartholomew, the spiritual leader of 300 million Orthodox Christians around the world, was lauded for "outstanding and enduring contributions to religious understanding and peace." Nelson Rolihlahla Mandela was cited for his "lifelong dedication to the abolition of apartheid and promotion of reconciliation among the people of the Republic of South Africa."[76]

Congress honored Father Theodore M. Hesburgh, President of the University of Notre Dame from 1952 until 1987, for his "outstanding and enduring contributions to civil rights, higher education, the Catholic Church, the Nation, and the global community." John Cardinal O'Connor, Archbishop of New York, was recognized for "his accomplishments as a priest, a Navy chaplain, and a humanitarian." Tribute was paid to Pope Paul II for "his many and enduring contributions to peace and religious understanding."[77]

Enduring and outstanding contributions to peace, non-violence, human rights, and religion won acclaim for Tenzin Gyatso, the Fourteenth Dalai Lama. Recognition was bestowed on Daw Aung San Suu Kyi for "her courageous and unwavering commitment to peace, nonviolence, human rights, and democracy in Burma."[78] Dr. Muhammad Yunus was recognized for his "contributions to the fight against global poverty."[79]

These recent awards are not without precedent, since the first and only Gold Medal given to an organization honored the American Red Cross in 1979 for "unselfish and humanitarian service to the people of the United States." [80]

Foreign Recipients

Thirty-one of the Congressional Gold Medals authorized to date have gone to non-Americans. In 1847, 10 officers and men belonging to or attached to French, British, and Spanish ships-of-war in the harbor of Vera Cruz captured congressional attention for aiding in the rescue of officers and crew of the United States brig *Somers*.[81] Eight years after Congress paid tribute to Dr. Frederick A. Rose of the British Navy in 1858,[82] Captain Robert Creighton, of the British ship *Three Bells,* won acclaim for aiding in the rescue of survivors from the steamship *San Francisco*. [83]

Gold medals were also given to Señor Domicio da Gama, Señor Rómulo S. Naón, and Señor Eduardo Suárez, the diplomatic representatives of Argentina, Brazil, and Chile who acted as mediators between the United States and Mexico in 1914;[84] and to Norwegian explorer Roald Amundsen and Italian explorer Umberto Nobile for their participation in American explorer Lincoln Ellsworth's polar flight of 1925 and his 1926 transpolar flight.[85]

In 1969, President Nixon was authorized to present a gold medal in the name of the United States and in the name of Congress to the widow of the late British Prime Minister Winston Churchill.[86]

Canadian Ambassador to Iran Kenneth Taylor was honored in March 1980 for his efforts in securing the safe return of six American Embassy officials in their escape from Tehran.[87]

Congress recognized Simon Wiesenthal of Austria in 1980 for his dedicated action in bringing to justice Nazi war criminals who had gone into hiding at the end of World War II.[88] Early in 1982, Her Majesty Queen Beatrix of the Netherlands was awarded a gold medal in recognition of the bicentennial anniversary of diplomatic and commercial relations between her country and the United States.[89] Natan (Anatoly) and Avital Shcharansky of the former Soviet Union were applauded in 1986 for their "supreme dedication and total commitment to the cause of individual human rights and freedoms."[90]

During the 105th Congress, the President was authorized to award gold medals to three additional foreign recipients—Mother Teresa of Calcutta,

Ecumenical Patriarch Bartholomew, a Turkish citizen, and Nelson Rolihlahla Mandela of the Republic of South Africa.[91] In the 106th Congress, Pope John Paul II was cited.[92] British Prime Minister Tony Blair in 2003 became the first Briton since Winston Churchill to be awarded the Congressional Gold Medal.[93] Three years later, Tenzin Gyatso, Tenzin, the Fourteenth Dalai Lama, earned recognition.[94] Daw Aung San Suu Kyi of Burma won acclaim in 2008, as did Dr. Muhammad Yunus in 2010.[95] In 2012, a Congressional Gold Medal was awarded to Raoul Wallenberg in recognition of his achievements and heroic actions during the Holocaust.[96]

DESIGN AND CASTING OF GOLD MEDALS

After a Congressional Gold Medal bill has been approved by both houses of Congress and signed into law by the President, officials of the United States Mint meet with the sponsors of the legislation and members of the honoree's family to discuss possible designs for the medal. Photographs of the honoree are also examined during this meeting. Mint engravers then prepare a series of sketches of possible designs for consideration and comment by the Commission of Fine Arts[97] and subsequently the Secretary of the Treasury, who makes the final decision on the medal's design. Once the Secretary of the Treasury, in consultation with the honoree's family, has made a selection, the design is sculptured, a die is made, and the medal is struck at the Philadelphia Mint. The Mint then notifies the White House and arrangements are made for a formal presentation by the President.[98]

The cost of issuing a Congressional Gold Medal, generally about $30,000, is charged against the United States Mint Public Enterprise Fund. Congress established this revolving fund "in the Treasury of the United States ... to be available to the Secretary for numismatic operations and programs of the United States Mint without fiscal year limitations."[99] The authorizing legislation in each case typically includes a provision stating that the "Secretary may strike and sell duplicates in bronze of the gold medal struck ... at a price sufficient to cover the costs of the medals (including labor, materials, dies, use of machinery, and overhead expenses) and the cost of the gold medal."[100] Monies received from the sales of the bronze duplicates are deposited in the United States Mint Public Enterprise Fund.[101]

LEGISLATIVE PROCEDURES

Procedures in the 113th Congress

In the 113th Congress, Rule 3(f)(1)(A) of the House Committee on Financial Services stipulates that the Subcommittee on Domestic Monetary Policy and Technology will not hold a hearing on Congressional Gold Medal legislation unless it is cosponsored by at least two-thirds (290) of the Members of the House. Rule 3(f)(1)(C) requires the subcommittee to apply the following standards in considering legislation authorizing Congressional Gold Medals:

- the recipient shall be a natural person;
- the recipient shall have performed an achievement that has an impact on American history and culture that is likely to be recognized as a major achievement in the recipient's field long after the achievement;
- the recipient shall not have received a medal previously for the same or substantially the same achievement;
- the recipient shall be living or, if deceased, shall have been deceased for not less than five years and not more than 25 years; and
- the achievements were performed in the recipient's field of endeavor, and represent either a lifetime of continuous superior achievements or a single achievement so significant that the recipient is recognized and acclaimed by others in the same field, as evidenced by the recipient having received the highest honors in the field.[102]

The Senate Banking, Housing, and Urban Affairs Committee in the 113th Congress requires that at least 67 Senators must cosponsor any Congressional Gold Medal bill before the committee will consider it.[103]

Statutory Limitations on Eligibility

Although Congress has approved legislation stipulating requirements for numerous other awards and decorations,[104] there are no permanent statutory provisions specifically relating to the creation of Congressional Gold Medals. When a Congressional Gold Medal has been deemed appropriate, Congress has, by legislative action, provided for the creation of a medal on an *ad hoc* basis.

Statutory Limitations on Awarding or Striking Gold Medals

CRS research did not identify any statutory restrictions on the number of gold medals that may be awarded by Congress or struck by the U.S. Mint. Furthermore, since each award made by Congress is itself statutory law, it is unlikely that any statutory limitation on the annual number of Congressional Gold Medals that could be struck would prevent the enactment of legislation authorizing additional medals.

Party Rules Related to Gold Medals

The rules of the House Republican Conference place an indirect restriction on the number of gold medals that may be awarded annually. Rule 28(a)(7) prohibits the Republican leader from scheduling, or requesting to have scheduled, any bill for consideration under suspension of the rules which "directs the Secretary of the Treasury to strike an additional Congressional Gold Medal in a particular calendar year if the Secretary has already been directed to strike 2 medals in such year."[105] A waiver on the restriction can be granted by the majority of the elected leadership of the conference.[106] In addition, because the restriction only applies to bills considered under suspension of the rules, it appears that an otherwise-prohibited bill could be brought to the floor under an alternative procedure, such as a special rule.

Bills to Change Procedures or Criteria

As of this writing, there have been no proposals in the 113th Congress to change the procedures or criteria for awarding congressional gold medals. During the 109th Congress, however, on January 26, 2005, the House, by a vote of 231 to 173, approved H.R. 54, the Congressional Gold Medal Enhancement Act of 2005, sponsored by Representative Michael N. Castle. The bill would have amended Section 5111 of Title 31 of the *United States Code* by adding the following new subsection:

(e) Congressional Gold Medal Standards—

(1) MAXIMUM NUMBER—Beginning on the date of the enactment of the Congressional Gold Medal Enhancement Act of 2005, the Secretary of the Treasury may strike not more than 2 congressional

gold medals for presentation pursuant to an Act of the Congress in any calendar year.

(2) PROGRAM REQUIREMENTS—The Secretary may strike congressional gold medals only in accordance with the following requirements:

(A) RECIPIENTS—Only an individual may be a recipient of a congressional gold medal.

(B) TIMING—No gold medal may be presented posthumously on behalf of any individual except during the 20-year period beginning 5 years after the death of the individual (unless the Act of Congress authorizing the striking of such medal was enacted before the death of such individual).

During House debate on H.R. 54, Representative Castle emphasized that his measure sought "to maintain the prestige of the medal by limiting the number that may be awarded each year," and to "clarify that recipients are individuals and not groups." Passage of the measure, he argued, "will ensure the future integrity and true honor of the award. It is my goal that every recipient, [P]resident, civil rights leader, military hero, inventor, or noted healer, who receives the Congressional Gold Medal will remain part of a unique honor bestowed by the United States Congress."[107]

House Financial Services Committee Chairman Michael G. Oxley characterized the proposed legislation as a "commonsense effort to maintain the prestige of this award." By limiting the number of medals that can be struck each year, and by "limiting the recipients to individuals rather than groups, maintains the prestige and honor of receiving a Congressional Gold Medal. Combined with the requirement of a minimum co-sponsorship level of two-thirds of the House is the best way to preserve the integrity of the gold medal."[108]

Representative Joseph Crowley in opposing the legislation told his House colleagues, "We are rushing to act on an issue that does not represent a problem." "Who that received this medal in the past," he asked, "was not worthy of it?" He also expressed dismay "that the Committee on Rules refused to allow consideration of a key amendment that would strike a section of bill that only permits the granting of Congressional Gold Medals to individuals." Although Crowley tended "to agree with the notion that distributing what is an exceptional honor to too many individuals could devalue the symbolic worth of a gold medal, there are occasions when more than one person is justified to receive the medal for their honorable actions in tandem with others." He continued by emphasizing that had this bill already been law, "Congress would not have been able to issue" a Congressional Gold Medal "to the Little Rock Nine," to "President and Mrs. Reagan," or to "Martin Luther King and Coretta Scott King."[109]

The House adopted by voice vote an amendment to H.R. 54 offered by Representative Oxley that would make the legislation effective immediately upon passage, instead of the original effective date of January 1, 2006. Two amendments offered by Representative Crowley, both of which were defeated, would have (1) raised the number of Gold Medals that could be approved from two per calendar year to six per Congress, or an overall increase of two medals per Congress; and (2) required that there be an equitable distribution of Gold Medals approved between those sponsored by the majority and minority parties.[110]

Later the same day, H.R. 54 was received in the Senate, read twice, and referred to the Senate Committee on Banking, Housing, and Urban Affairs. There was no further action on the bill.

Appendix. Recipients of Congressional Gold Medals, 1776-2012: A Chronological List

George Washington. In recognition of the "wise and spirited conduct" of George Washington, and the officers and soldiers under his command, in the siege and acquisition of Boston. Approved March 25, 1776 (U.S. Continental Congress, *Journal of the Continental Congress 1774-1789,* 34 vols. (Washington: GPO, 1906, vol. 4, p. 234).

Major General Horatio Gates. In recognition of the "brave and successful efforts" of Major General Horatio Gates, commander in chief in the northern department, and Major General Benjamin Lincoln and Major General Benedict Arnold, and the other officers and troops under his command, "in support of the independence of their country at Saratoga." Approved November 4, 1777 (*Journal of the Continental Congress 1774-1789*, vol. 9, pp. 861-862).

Major General Anthony Wayne. In recognition of the "good conduct, coolness, discipline, and firm intrepidity" of Major General Anthony Wayne, and the officers and soldiers under his command, in the assault of the enemy's works at Stony Point. Approved July 26, 1779 (*Journal of the Continental Congress 1774-1789*, vol. 14, p. 890).

Major Henry Lee. In recognition of the "remarkable prudence, address and bravery" exhibited by Major Henry Lee, and the non-commissioned officers and soldiers under his command, for their surprise raid of Pawles (Paulus) Hook, NJ, in August 1779. Approved September 24, 1779 (*Journal of the Continental Congress 1774-1789*, vol. 15, pp. 1099-1102).

Brigadier General Daniel Morgan. In recognition of the "fortitude and good conduct" displayed by Brigadier General Daniel Morgan, and the officers and men under his command, in the action at Cowpens, in the state of South Carolina on January 17, 1781. Approved March 9, 1781 (*Journal of the Continental Congress 1774-1789*, vol. 19, pp. 246-247).

Major General Nathaniel Greene. In recognition of Major General Nathaniel Greene's "wise, decisive and magnanimous conduct in the action" of September 8, 1781, "near Eutaw Springs, in South Carolina; in which, with a force inferior in number to that of the enemy, he obtained a most signal victory." Approved October 29, 1781 (*Journal of the Continental Congress*, 1774-1789, vol. 21, pp. 1083-1084).

John Paul Jones. In recognition of the "valor and brilliant services" of John Paul Jones in commanding a "squadron of French and American ships under the flag and commission of the United States off the coast of Great Britain." Approved October 16, 1787 (*Journal of the Continental Congress 1774-1789*, vol. 33, p. 687).

Captain Thomas Truxtun. In recognition of the "gallantry and good conduct" of Captain Thomas Truxtun in the action between the United States frigate *Constellation* and the French ship of war *La Vengeance*. Approved March 29, 1800 (2 Stat. 87).

Commodore Edward Preble. In recognition of the "gallantry and good conduct" displayed by Captain Edward Preble, and the officers, petty officers, seamen and marines attached to the squadron under his command, in the several attacks on the town, batteries, and naval force of Tripoli in 1804. Approved March 3, 1805 (2 Stat. 346-347).

Captain Isaac Hull, Captain Stephen Decatur, and Captain Jacob Jones. In recognition of the "gallantry, good conduct, and services" of Captain Isaac Hull of the frigate *Constitution*, Captain Stephen Decatur of the frigate *United States*, and Captain Jacob Jones of the sloop-of-war *Wasp*, in their respective conflicts with the British frigates the *Guerriere* and the *Macedonian*, and sloop-of-war *Frolic*. Approved January 29, 1813 (2 Stat. 830).

Captain William Bainbridge. In recognition of the "gallantry, good conduct and services of Captain William Bainbridge," and the officers and crew of the frigate *Constitution*, in the capture of the British frigate *Java*, after a "brave and skillful combat." Approved March 3, 1813 (2 Stat. 831).

Captain Oliver Hazard Perry and Captain Jesse D. Elliott. In recognition of the "decisive and glorious victory gained on Lake Erie" by Captain Oliver Hazard Perry and Captain Jesse D. Elliott, on September 10, 1813. Approved January 6, 1814 (3 Stat. 141).

Lieutenant William Burrows and Lieutenant Edward R. M'Call. In recognition of the "gallantry and good conduct" of Lieutenant William Burrows and Lieutenant Edward R. M'Call of the brig *Enterprise*, in the conflict with the British sloop *Boxer* on September 4, 1813. Approved January 6, 1814 (3 Stat. 141-142).

Captain James Lawrence. In recognition of the "gallantry and good conduct" of Captain James Lawrence, and the officers and crew of the sloop-of-war *Hornet*, in the capture of the British vessel of war, the *Peacock*. Approved January 11, 1814 (3 Stat. 142).

Captain Thomas MacDonough, Captain Robert Henly, and Lieutenant Stephen Cassin. In recognition of the "decisive and splendid victory" of Captain Thomas MacDonough and Lieutenant Stephen Cassin, gained on Lake Champlain on September 11, 1814. Approved October 20, 1814 (3 Stat. 245-246).

Captain Lewis Warrington. In recognition of the "gallantry and good conduct" of Captain Lewis Warrington, and the officers and crew of the sloop-of-war *Peacock* in the action with the British brig *Epervier* on April 29, 1814. Approved October 21, 1814 (3 Stat. 246).

Captain Johnston Blakely. In recognition of the "gallantry and good conduct" of Captain Johnston Blakely, and the officers and crew of the sloop *Wasp* in the action with the British sloop- of-war *Reindeer* on June 28, 1814. Approved November 3, 1814 (3 Stat. 246-247).

Major General Jacob Brown. In recognition of the "gallantry and good conduct" of Major General Jacob Brown, and the "officers and men, of the regular army, and of the militia under his command ... in the successive battles of Chippewa, Niagara, and Erie, in Upper Canada, in which British veteran soldiers were beaten and repulsed by equal and inferior numbers." Approved November 3, 1814 (3 Stat. 247).

Major General Winfield Scott. In recognition of the "uniform gallantry and good conduct" of Major General Winfield Scott "in the successive conflicts of Chippewa and Niagara." Approved November 3, 1814 (3 Stat. 247).

Brigadier General Eleazar W. Ripley, Brigadier General James Miller, and Major General Peter B. Porter. In recognition of the "gallantry and good conduct" of Brigadier General Eleazar W. Ripley, Brigadier General James Miller, and Major General Peter B. Porter "in the several conflicts of Chippewa, Niagara, and Erie." Approved November 3, 1814 (3 Stat. 247).

Major General Edmund P. Gaines. In recognition of the "gallantry and good conduct" of General Edmund P. Gaines, and the officers and men under his command, in defeating the British army at Erie on August 15, 1814. Approved November 3, 1814 (3 Stat. 247).

Major General Alexander Macomb. In recognition of the "gallantry and good conduct" of Major General Alexander Macomb, and the officers and men under his command, in defeating a veteran British army at Plattsburg on September 11, 1814. Approved November 3, 1814 (3 Stat. 247).

Major General Andrew Jackson. In recognition of the "valor, skill and good conduct" of Major General Andrew Jackson, and the officers and soldiers of the regular army, of the militia, and of the volunteers under his command, which was conspicuously displayed against the British army at New Orleans on January 8, 1815. Approved February 27, 1815 (3 Stat. 249).

Captain Charles Stewart. In recognition of the "gallantry, good conduct and services" of Captain Charles Stewart, and the officers and crew, of the frigate *Constitution*, in capturing the British vessels of war, the *Cyane* and the *Levant,* after a brave and skillful combat. Approved February 22, 1816 (3 Stat. 341).

Captain James Biddle. In recognition of the "gallantry, good conduct and services" of Captain James Biddle, and the officers and crew, of the sloop-of-war *Hornet*, in capturing the British sloop-of-war *Penguin*, after a brave and skillful combat. Approved February 22, 1816 (3 Stat. 341).

Major General William Henry Harrison and Governor Isaac Shelby. In recognition of the "gallantry and good behavior" of Major William Henry Harrison and Governor Isaac Shelby, and the officers and men under their command, "in defeating the combined British and Indian forces under Major General Proctor, on the Thames, in Upper Canada, on October 5, 1813, and in capturing the British army with their baggage, camp equipage and artillery." Approved April 4, 1818 (3 Stat. 476).

Colonel George Croghan. In recognition of the "gallantry and good conduct" of Colonel George Croghan in the defense of Fort Stephenson in 1813. Approved February 13, 1835 (4 Stat. 792).

Major General Zachary Taylor. In recognition of the "fortitude, skill, enterprise, and courage" of Major General Zachary Taylor, and his officers and men, which distinguished the brilliant operations on the Rio Grande. Approved July 16, 1846 (9 Stat. 111).

Major General Zachary Taylor. In recognition of the "fortitude, skill, enterprise, and courage" of Major General Zachary Taylor, and his officers and men, which distinguished the brilliant military operations at Monterey. Approved March 2, 1847 (9 Stat. 206).

Rescuers of the Officers and Crew of the U. S. Brig Somers. In recognition of the "officers and men belonging or attached to the French, British, and Spanish ships-of-war in the harbor of Vera Cruz, who so gallantly, and at the imminent peril of their lives, aided rescuing from a watery grave many of the officers and crew of the United States brig *Somers*." The records of the United States Mint indicate that 10 gold medals were struck in commemoration of the gallant effort of the *Somers*. Approved March 3, 1847 (9 Stat. 208).

Major General Winfield Scott. In recognition of the "uniform gallantry and good conduct" of Major General Winfield Scott, and the officers and men of the regular and volunteer corps under him, "conspicuously displayed at the siege and capture of the city of Vera Cruz and castle of San Juan de Ulloa," on March 29, 1847; in the successive battles of Cerro Gordo on April 18, San Antonio and Churubusco on August 19 and 20; in the "victories achieved in front of the city of Mexico" on September 8 and 11-13; and for the capture of the metropolis on September 14, "in which the Mexican troops, greatly superior in numbers, and with every advantage of position, were in every conflict signally defeated by the American arms." Approved March 9, 1848 (9 Stat. 333).

Major General Zachary Taylor. In recognition of the "valor, skill, and good conduct" of Major General Zachary Taylor, and the officers and soldiers of the regular army and of the volunteers under his command, "conspicuously displayed" on February 22 and 23, 1848, in the battle of Buena Vista, in "defeating a Mexican army under the command of General Santa Anna of more than four times their number." Approved May 9, 1848 (9 Stat. 334-335).

Commander Duncan N. Ingraham. In recognition of the "gallant and judicious conduct" of Commander Duncan N. Ingraham "in extending protection to Martin Koszta, by rescuing him from illegal seizure and imprisonment on board the Austrian war-brig *Hussar*." Approved August 4, 1854 (10 Stat. 594-595).

Frederick A. Rose. In recognition of "Assistant-Surgeon Frederick A. Rose, of the British navy, who volunteered, with the permission of his commanding officer, to join the *Susquehannah*," at a time when many of its crew had yellow fever, "at imminent personal risk, devoted himself, on the voyage from Jamaica to New York, to care for the sick remaining on board." Approved May 11, 1858 (11 Stat. 369).

Major General Ulysses S. Grant. In recognition of "gallantry and good conduct" of Ulysses S. Grant, and the officers and men who fought under his command during the Civil War, in the battles in which they engaged. Approved December 17, 1863 (13 Stat. 399).

Cornelius Vanderbilt. In recognition of Cornelius Vanderbilt's "gift to his imperiled country" of the steamship *Vanderbilt*, which was "actively employed in the service of the Republic against the rebel devastations of her commerce." Approved January 28, 1864 (13 Stat. 401).

Captains Robert Creighton, Edwin J. Low, and George C. Stouffer. In recognition of the "gallant conduct" of Captain Robert Creighton, of the ship *Three Bells*, of Glasgow; Captain Edwin J. Low, of the bark *Kilby*, of Boston; and Captain George C. Stouffer, of the ship *Antarctic,* in rescuing about 500 men from the wreck of the steamer *San Francisco*. Approved July 26, 1866 (14 Stat. 365-366).

Cyrus W. Field. In recognition of the "foresight, courage, and determination" of Cyrus W. Field "in establishing telegraphic communications by means of the Atlantic cable traversing mid-ocean and connecting the Old World with the New." Approved March 2, 1867 (14 Stat. 574).

George Peabody. In recognition of George Peabody's "great and peculiar beneficence" in giving $2 million "for the promotion of education in the most destitute portions of the southern and southwestern States." Approved March 16, 1867 (15 Stat. 20).

George F. Robinson. In recognition of the "heroic conduct" of George F. Robinson in saving the life of Secretary of State William H. Seward on April 14, 1865. Approved March 1, 1871 (16 Stat. 704).

Captain Jared S. Crandall, and Others. In recognition of the services of Captain Jared S. Crandall, Albert Crandall, Daniel F. Larkin, Frank Larkin, Bryon Green, John D. Harvey, Courtland Gavitt, Eugene Nash, Edwin Nash, and William Nash of Westerly, RI, who "so gallantly volunteered to man a life-boat and a fishing-boat, and saved the lives of thirty-two persons from the wreck of the steamer *Metis* on the waters of the Long Island sound," on August 31, 1872. Approved February 24, 1873 (17 Stat. 638).

John Horn, Jr. In recognition and commemoration of the "heroic and humane exploits" of John Horn, Jr., in rescuing 110 men, women, and children from drowning in the Detroit River. Approved June 20, 1874 (18 Stat. 573).

On April 28, 1904, Congress authorized and directed the Secretary of the Treasury to strike off and present to John Horn, Jr., a duplicate of the medal voted by Congress to him in 1874, which was stolen from him in October 1901. Approved April 28, 1904 (33 Stat. 1684-1685).

John F. Slater. In recognition of John F. Slater's contribution of $1 million for the purpose of "uplifting the lately emancipated population of the Southern States and their prosperity, by conferring on them the blessings of Christian education." Approved February 5, 1883 (22 Stat. 636).

Joseph Francis. In recognition of Joseph Francis' "life-long services to humanity and to his country ... in the construction and perfection of life-saving appliances by which thousands of lives have been saved." Approved August 27, 1888 (25 Stat. 1249).

Chief Engineer George Wallace Melville and Others. In recognition of the "meritorious service" of Chief Engineer George Wallace Melville, United States Navy, "in successfully directing the party under his command after the wreck of the Arctic exploring steamer *Jeannette*, and of his persistent efforts through dangers and hardships to find and assist his commanding officer and other members of the expedition before he himself was out of peril." This act does not specifically indicate what type of medal was to be presented to Chief Engineer Melville and the officers and men of the *Jeannette* "as an expression of the high esteem Congress [held] their services." The records of the United States Mint, however, indicate that eight gold medals were struck in commemoration of the perils encountered by the *Jeannette* expedition. Approved September 30, 1890 (26 Stat. 552-553).

First Lieutenant Frank H. Newcomb. In recognition of the "intrepid and heroic gallantry" of First Lieutenant Frank H. Newcomb, commander of the revenue cutter *Hudson*, and the officers and men under his command, "in action at Cardenas, Cuba," on May 18, 1898, "when the *Hudson* rescued the United States naval torpedo boat *Winslow* in the face of a most galling fire from the enemy's guns, the *Winslow* being disabled, her captain wounded, her only other officer and half her crew killed." Approved May 3, 1900 (31 Stat. 717).

First Lieutenant David H. Jarvis, Second Lieutenant Ellsworth P. Bertholf, and Dr. Samuel J. Call. In recognition of the "heroic service" rendered by First Lieutenant David H. Jarvis, Second Lieutenant Ellsworth P. Bertholf, and Dr. Samuel J. Call, all of the Revenue-Cutter Service and members of the overland expedition of 1897-1898, in providing relief to the whaling fleet in arctic regions. Approved June 28, 1902 (32 Stat. 492).

Wright Brothers. In recognition and appreciation of the "great service" Orville and Wilbur Wright of Ohio, "rendered the science of aerial navigation in the invention of the Wright aeroplane, and for their ability, courage, and success in navigating the air." Approved March 4, 1909 (35 Stat. 1627).

Captain Arthur Henry Rostron. In recognition of Captain Henry Rostron, and the officers and crew of the steamship *Carpathia*, "for promptly going to the relief of the steamship *Titanic* and heroically saving the lives of seven hundred and four people who had been shipwrecked in the North Atlantic Ocean." Approved July 6, 1912 (37 Stat. 639).

Captain Paul H. Kreibohm and Others. In recognition of the heroic rescue of 89 people by Captain Paul H. Kreibohm and the officers and crew of the American steamer *Kroonland* from the burning steamer *Volturno* in the North Atlantic. The records of the United States Mint indicate that four gold medals were struck in commemoration of the actions of the *Kroonland*. Approved March 19, 1914 (38 Stat. 769).

Señor Domicio da Gama, Señor Rómulo S. Naón, and Señor Eduardo Suárez. In recognition of the "generous services" of Señor Domicio da Gama, Señor Rómulo S. Naón, and Señor Eduardo Suárez, "as mediators in the controversy between the Government of the United States and the leaders of the warring parties in the Republic of Mexico." Approved March 4, 1915 (38 Stat. 1228).

Charles A. Lindbergh. In recognition of the "achievements" of Charles A. Lindbergh. Approved May 4, 1928 (45 Stat. 490).

Lincoln Ellsworth, Roald Amundsen, and Umberto Nobile. In recognition of the "conspicuous courage, sagacity, and perseverance" Lincoln Ellsworth exhibited during his famous polar flight of 1925 and his transpolar flight of 1926; and the contributions of Roald Amundsen, the distinguished Norwegian explorer, and Umberto Nobile, the distinguished Italian explorer, who participated with Ellsworth in the transpolar flight of 1926. Approved May 29, 1928 (45 Stat. 2026-2027).

Thomas A. Edison. In recognition of the "achievements" of Thomas A. Edison. Approved May 29, 1928 (45 Stat. 1012).

First Successful Trans-Atlantic Flight. In recognition of Commander John H. Tower's "extraordinary achievement" in conceiving, organizing, and commanding the first trans-Atlantic flight; and Lieutenant Commander Albert C. Read, United States Navy, commanding officer; Lieutenant Elmer F. Stone, United States Coast Guard, pilot; Lieutenant Walter Hinton, United States Navy, pilot; Lieutenant H. C. Rodd, United States Navy, radio operator; Lieutenant J. L. Breese, United States Naval Reserve Force, engineer; and Machinist's Mate Eugene Rhodes, United States Navy, engineer, "in making the first successful trans-Atlantic flight, in the United States naval flying boat NC-4, in May 1919." Approved February 9, 1929 (45 Stat. 1158).

Major Walter Reed and Associates for Yellow Fever Experimentations in Cuba. In recognition of the "high public service rendered and disabilities contracted" by Major Walter Reed, James Carroll, Jesse W. Lazear, Aristides Agramonte, James A. Andrus, John R. Bullard, A. W. Covington, William H. Dean, Wallace W. Forbes, Levi E. Folk, Paul Hamann, James F. Hanberry, Warren G. Jernegan, John R. Kissinger, John J. Moran, William Olsen, Charles G. Sonntag, Clyde L. West, Dr. R. P. Cooke, Thomas M. England, James Hildebrand, and Edward Weatherwalks "in the interest of humanity and science as voluntary subjects for the experimentation during the yellow-fever investigations in Cuba." Approved February 28, 1929 (45 Stat. 1409-1410).

This act was subsequently amended on July 2, 1956, and September 2, 1958, to include the names of Gustaf E. Lambert and Roger P. Ames (70 Stat. 484; and 72 Stat. 1702).

Officers and Men of the Byrd Antarctic Expedition. In recognition of the "high admiration in which Congress and the American people hold [the] heroic and undaunted services [connected] with the scientific investigations and extraordinary aerial expeditions of the Antarctic Continent, under the personal direction of Rear Admiral Richard E. Byrd." The records of the United States Mint indicate that 67 gold medals were struck in commemoration of the Byrd Antarctic Expedition. Approved May 23, 1930 (46 Stat. 379).

Lincoln Ellsworth. In recognition of Lincoln Ellsworth "claiming on behalf of the United States approximately three-hundred-fifty-thousand square miles of land in the Antarctic between the eightieth and one hundred and twentieth meridians west of Greenwich, representing the last unclaimed territory in the world, and for his exceptionally meritorious services to science and aeronautics in making a two-thousand-five-hundred mile aerial survey of the heart of Antarctica, thus paving the way for more detailed studies of geological, meteorological, and geographical questions of world-wide importance and benefit." Approved June 16, 1936 (49 Stat. 2324).

George M. Cohan. In recognition of the public service of George M. Cohan during the World War in composing the patriotic songs "Over There" and "A Grand Old Flag." Approved June 29, 1936 (49 Stat. 2371).

Mrs. Richard Aldrich and Anna Bouligny. In recognition of Mrs. Richard Aldrich and Anna Bouligny "who, during the War with Spain, voluntarily went to Puerto Rico and there rendered service of inestimable value to the Army of the United States in the establishment and operation of hospitals for the care and treatment of military patients in Puerto Rico." Approved June 20, 1938 (52 Stat. 1365).

Howard Hughes. In recognition of the "achievements" of Howard Hughes in "advancing the science of aviation and thus bringing great credit to his country throughout the world." Approved August 7, 1939 (53 Stat. 1525).

Reverend Francis X. Quinn. In recognition of the "valor of Reverend Francis X. Quinn, pastor of the Church of the Guardian Angel, New York City, who risked his life by entering the room when an armed desperado held two elderly persons as hostages, and who by successfully disarming this criminal and saving the lives of two innocent persons distinguished himself conspicuously by gallantry and intrepidity at the risk of his life above and beyond the call of his duty." Approved August 10, 1939 (53 Stat. 1533).

William Sinnott. In recognition of action of "William Sinnott, a detective, who in guarding Franklin D. Roosevelt, then President-elect of the United States, at Miami, Florida, on February 15, 1933, was shot and wounded by Giuseppe Zangara, who attempted to assassinate" Mr. Roosevelt. Approved June 15, 1940 (54 Stat. 1283).

Roland Boucher. In recognition of the "valor, bravery, and heroism of Roland Boucher, of Burlington, Vermont, age 11, who on February 12, 1941, risked his life in rescuing five children who had broken through the ice on Lake Champlain near Juniper Island, saving the lives of four, and who in so doing displayed unusual bravery and the presence of mind extraordinary in one of his age." Approved January 20, 1942 (56 Stat. 1099-1100).

General of the Army George Catlett Marshall and Fleet Admiral Ernest Joseph King. In recognition of General of the Army George C. Marshall's "distinguished leadership, as Chief of Staff of the Army and as a member of the Combined Chiefs of Staff of the United Nations, in planning the expansion, equipment, training and deployment of the great Army of the United States and in formulating and executing the global strategy that led to victory in World War II," and the "members of the Army of the United States who served under his direction with such heroic devotion, and personal sacrifice."

In recognition also of Admiral Ernest J. King's "distinguished leadership as Commander in Chief of the United States Fleet and Chief of Naval Operations and as a member of the Combined Chiefs of Staff of the United Nations, in planning the expansion, equipment, training, and operation of the United States Navy and in formulating and executing the global strategy that led to victory in World War II," and the "members of the United States Navy, the United States Marine Corps and the United States Coast Guard," and the "members of the Reserve Forces who served under his direction with such heroic devotion and personal sacrifice." Approved March 22, 1946 (60 Stat. 1134-1135).

General of the Armies of the United States John J. Pershing. In recognition of General John J. Pershing's "peerless leadership, heroic achievements, and great military victories, as Commander in Chief of the American Expeditionary Forces in Europe in World War I, and for his gallant and unselfish devotion to the service of his country in preparation for, and the prosecution of World War II." Approved August 7, 1946 (60 Stat. 1297-1298).

Brigadier General William Mitchell. In recognition of the "outstanding pioneer service and foresight of General William Mitchell in the field of American military aviation." Approved August 8, 1946 (60 Stat. 1319).

Vice President Alben W. Barkley. In recognition of Vice President Alben W. Barkley's "distinguished public service and outstanding contribution to the general welfare." Approved August 12, 1949 (P.L. 81-221, 63 Stat. 599).

Irving Berlin. In recognition of Irvin Berlin's "services in composing many patriotic songs, including God Bless America, which became popular during World War II." Approved July 16, 1954 (P.L. 83-536, 68 Stat. A120).

Doctor Jonas E. Salk. "In recognition of the great achievement of Doctor Jonas E. Salk in the field of medicine by his discovery of a serum for the prevention of poliomyelitis." Approved August 9, 1955 (P.L. 84-297, 69 Stat. 589).

Surviving Veterans of the War Between the States. "In honor of the last [four] surviving veterans of the War Between the States who served in the Union or the Confederate forces." Approved July 18, 1956 (P.L. 84-730, 70 Stat. 577).

Rear Admiral Hyman George Rickover. "In recognition of the achievements of Rear Admiral Hyman George Rickover, United States Navy, in successfully directing the development and construction of the world's first nuclear-powered ships and the first large-scale nuclear power reactor devoted exclusively to the production of electricity." Approved August 28, 1958 (P.L. 85- 826, 72 Stat. 985).

Doctor Robert H. Goddard. In recognition of the "great, creative achievements of Doctor Robert H. Goddard, and his historic pioneering research on space rockets, missiles, and jet propulsion." Approved September 16, 1959 (P.L. 86-277, 73 Stat. 562-563).

Robert Frost. In recognition of Robert Frost's "poetry, which has enriched the culture of the United States and the philosophy of the world." Approved September 13, 1960 (P.L. 86-747, 74 Stat. 883).

Doctor Thomas Anthony Dooley III. "In recognition of the gallant and unselfish public service rendered by Doctor Thomas Anthony Dooley III in serving the medical needs of the people of Laos living in the remote areas of the Laotian jungles, and the peoples in other newly developing countries." Approved May 27, 1961 (P.L. 87-42, 75 Stat. 87).

Bob Hope. In recognition of Bob Hope's outstanding "service to his country and the cause of peace." Approved June 8, 1962 (P.L. 87-478, 76 Stat. 93).

Sam Rayburn, Speaker of the House of Representatives. In recognition of Sam Rayburn's "distinguished public service and outstanding contribution to the general welfare." Approved September 26, 1962 (P.L. 87-702, 76 Stat. 605).

General of the Army Douglas MacArthur. "In recognition of the gallant service rendered by General of the Army Douglas MacArthur to his country." Approved October 9, 1962 (P.L. 87- 760, 76 Stat. 760).

Walt Disney. In recognition of Walt Disney's "distinguished public service and outstanding contributions to the United States and the world." Approved May 24, 1968 (P.L. 90-316, 82 Stat. 130-131).

Winston Churchill. In recognition of Winston Churchill, on the occasion of the dedication of the Winston Churchill Memorial and Library at Westminster College in Fulton, MO, in May 1969. Approved May 7, 1969 (P.L. 91-12, 83 Stat. 8-9).

Roberto Walker Clemente. In recognition of Roberto Clemente's "outstanding athletic, civil, charitable, and humanitarian contributions." Approved May 14, 1973 (P.L. 93-33, 87 Stat. 71).

Marian Anderson. "In recognition of the highly distinguished and impressive career of Miss Marian Anderson for a period of more than a half a century during which she has been the recipient of the highest awards from a score of foreign countries, for her untiring and unselfish devotion to the promotion of the arts in this country and throughout the world including the establishment of scholarships for young people, for her strong and imaginative support to humanitarian causes at home, for her contributions to the cause of world peace through her work as United States delegate to the United Nations and her performances and recordings which have reached an estimated seven million people throughout the world, and her unstinting efforts on behalf of the brotherhood of man, and the many treasured moments she has brought to us with enormous demand on her time, talent, and energy." Approved March 8, 1977 (P.L. 95-9, 91 Stat. 19).

Lieutenant General Ira C. Eaker. In recognition of Lieutenant General Ira C. Eaker's "distinguished career as an aviation pioneer and Air Force leader." Approved October 10, 1978 (P.L. 95-438, 92 Stat. 1060).

Robert F. Kennedy. In recognition of the "distinguished and dedicated service" Robert Kennedy "gave to the Government and to the people of the United States." Approved November 1, 1978 (P.L. 95-560, 92 Stat. 2142).

John Wayne. In recognition of John Wayne's "distinguished career as an actor and his service to the Nation." Approved May 26, 1979 (P.L. 96-15, 93 Stat. 32).

Ben Abruzzo, Maxie Anderson, and Larry Newman. In recognition of the "distinguished feat" of transatlantic balloonists Ben Abruzzo, Maxie Anderson, and Larry Newman "as aviation pioneers." Approved June 13, 1979 (P.L. 96-20, 93 Stat. 45).

Hubert H. Humphrey. In recognition of Hubert H. Humphrey's "distinguished and dedicated service" to the Government and to the people of the United States. Approved June 13, 1979 (P.L. 96-21, 93 Stat. 46).

American Red Cross. In recognition of the "unselfish and humanitarian service" of the American Red Cross to the people of the United States. Approved December 12, 1979 (P.L. 96- 138, 93 Stat. 1063).

Ambassador Kenneth Taylor. In recognition of Canadian Ambassador to Iran Kenneth Taylor's "valiant efforts to secure the safe return of six American Embassy officials in Tehran." Approved March 6, 1980 (P.L. 96-201, 94 Stat. 79).

Simon Wiesenthal. In recognition of Simon Wiesenthal's "contribution to international justice through the documentation and location of war criminals from World War II." Approved March 17, 1980 (P.L. 96-211, 94 Stat. 101).

Queen Beatrix of the Netherlands. In recognition of the "two hundredth anniversary, in 1982, of the establishment of diplomatic and commercial relations between the Governments of the United States and the Netherlands." Approved March 22, 1982 (P.L. 97-158, 96 Stat. 18-19).

Admiral Hyman George Rickover. In recognition of Admiral Hyman George Rickover's "distinguished service and for his unique world-renowned contributions to the development of safe nuclear energy and to the defense of the United States." Approved June 23, 1982 (P.L. 97- 201, 96 Stat. 126-127).

Fred Waring. In recognition of Fred Waring's "contribution to enriching American life." Approved August 26, 1982 (P.L. 97-246, 96 Stat. 315-316).

Joe Louis. In recognition of Joe Louis's "accomplishments which did so much to bolster the spirit of the American people during one of the most crucial times in American history and which have endured throughout the years as a symbol of strength for the Nation." Approved August 26, 1982 (P.L. 97-246, 96 Stat. 315-316).

Louis L'Amour. In recognition of Louis L'Amour's "distinguished career as an author and his contributions to the Nation through his historically based works." Approved August 26, 1982 (P.L. 97-246, 96 Stat. 315-316).

Leo J. Ryan. In recognition of Leo J. Ryan's "distinguished service as a Member of Congress and the fact of his untimely death by assassination while performing his responsibilities as a Member of the United States House of Representatives." Approved November 18, 1983 (P.L. 98- 159, 97 Stat. 992).

Danny Thomas. In recognition of Danny Thomas' "humanitarian efforts and his outstanding work as an American." Approved November 29, 1983 (P.L. 98-172, 97 Stat. 1119-1120).

Harry S. Truman. In recognition of the "life-time of outstanding public service which ... Harry S. Truman, gave to the United States, and in commemoration of his one hundredth birthday which was celebrated on May 8, 1984." Approved May 8, 1984 (P.L. 98-278, 98 Stat. 173-175).

Lady Bird Johnson. In recognition of Lady Bird Johnson's "humanitarian efforts and outstanding contributions to the improvement and beautification of America." Approved May 8, 1984 (P.L. 98-278, 98 Stat. 173-175).

Elie Wiesel. In recognition of Elie Wiesel's "humanitarian efforts and outstanding contributions to world literature and human rights." Approved May 8, 1984 (P.L. 98-278, 98 Stat. 173-175).

Roy Wilkins. In recognition of the "incomparable contribution of Roy Wilkins to the struggle for civil rights and equality for all Americans." Approved May 17, 1984 (P.L. 98-285, 98 Stat. 186).

George and Ira Gershwin. In recognition of "George and Ira Gershwin's outstanding and invaluable contributions to American music, theatre and culture." Approved August 9, 1985 (P.L. 99-86, 99 Stat. 288-289).

Natan (Anatoly) and Avital Shcharansky. In recognition of the "supreme dedication and total commitment" of Natan (Anatoly) and Avital Shcharansky "to the cause of individual human rights and freedoms." Approved May 13, 1986 (P.L. 99-298, 100 Stat. 432-433).

Harry Chapin. In recognition of "Harry Chapin's efforts to address issues of hunger around the world." Approved May 20, 1986 (P.L. 99-311, 100 Stat. 464).

Aaron Copland. In recognition of Aaron Copland's "contribution to American musical composition." Approved September 23, 1986 (P.L. 99-418, 100 Stat. 952-953).

Mary Lasker. In recognition of Mary Lasker's "humanitarian contributions in the areas of medical research and education, urban beautification and the fine arts." Approved December 24, 1987 (P.L. 100-210, 101 Stat. 1441).

Jesse Owens. In recognition of "Jesse Owens' athletic achievements and humanitarian contributions to public service, civil rights and international goodwill." Approved September 20, 1988 (P.L. 100-437, 102 Stat. 1717).

Andrew Wyeth. In recognition of Andrew Wyeth's "outstanding and invaluable contributions to American art and culture." Approved November 9, 1988 (P.L. 100-639, 102 Stat. 3331-3332).

Laurence Spelman Rockefeller. In recognition of Laurence Spelman Rockefeller's "leadership on behalf of natural resource conservation and historic preservation." Approved May 17, 1990 (P.L. 101-296, 104 Stat. 197-199).

General Matthew B. Ridgeway. In recognition of General Matthew B. Ridgeway's "distinguished service to the Nation" during World War II and the Korean War. Approved November 5, 1990 (P.L. 101-510; 104 Stat. 1720-1721).

General H. Norman Schwarzkopf. In recognition of General H. Norman Schwarzkopf's "exemplary performance as a military leader in coordinating the planning, strategy, and execution of the U.S. combat action and his invaluable contributions to the United States and to the liberation of Kuwait as Commander-in-Chief, United States Central Command." Approved April 23, 1991 (P.L. 102-32; 105 Stat. 175-176).

General Colin Powell. In recognition of General Colin Powell's "exemplary performance as a military leader and advisor to the President in planning and coordinating the military response of the United States to the Iraqi invasion of Kuwait and the ultimate retreat of Iraqi forces and Iraqi acceptance of all United Nations Resolutions relating to Kuwait." Approved April 23, 1991 (P.L. 102-33; 105 Stat. 177-178).

Rabbi Menachem Mendel Schneerson. In recognition of Rabbi Menachem Mendel Schneerson's "outstanding and enduring contributions toward world education, morality, and acts of charity." Approved November 2, 1994 (P.L. 103-457; 108 Stat. 4799-4800).

Ruth and Billy Graham. In recognition of Ruth and Billy Graham's "outstanding and lasting contributions to morality, racial equality, family, philanthropy, and religion." Approved February 13, 1996 (P.L. 104-111; 110 Stat. 772-773).

Francis Albert "Frank" Sinatra. In recognition of Frank Sinatra's "outstanding and enduring contributions through his entertainment career and humanitarian activities." Approved May 14, 1997 (P.L. 105-14, 111 Stat. 32-33).

Mother Teresa of Calcutta. In recognition of Mother Teresa of Calcutta's "outstanding and enduring contributions through humanitarian and charitable activities." Approved June 2, 1997 (P.L. 105-16, 111 Stat. 35-36).

Ecumenical Patriarch Bartholomew. In recognition of Ecumenical Patriarch Bartholomew's "outstanding and enduring contributions toward religious understanding and peace." Approved October 6, 1997 (P.L. 105-51, 111 Stat. 1170-1171).

Nelson Rolihlahla Mandela. In recognition of Nelson Rolihlahla's "life-long dedication to the abolition of apartheid and the promotion of reconciliation among the people of the Republic of South Africa." Approved July 29, 1998 (P.L. 105-215, 112 Stat. 895-896).

Little Rock Nine. In recognition of the "selfless heroism" Jean Brown Trickey, Carlotta Walls LaNier, Melba Patillo Beals, Terrence Roberts, Gloria Ray Karlmark, Thelma Mothershed Wair, Ernest Green, Elizabeth Eckford, and Jefferson Thomas "exhibited and the pain they suffered in the cause of civil rights by integrating Central High School in Little Rock, Arkansas." Approved October 21, 1998 (P.L. 105-277, 112 Stat. 2681-597).

Gerald R. and Betty Ford. In recognition of Gerald R. and Betty Ford's "dedicated public service and outstanding humanitarian contributions to the people of the United States." Approved October 21, 1998 (P.L. 105-277, 112 Stat. 2681-598).

Rosa Parks. In recognition of Rosa Parks' "contributions to the Nation" as the "first lady of civil rights" and "mother of the freedom movement," and whose "quiet dignity ignited the most significant social movement in the history of the United States." Approved May 4, 1999 (P.L. 106-26; 113 Stat. 50-51).

Theodore M. Hesburgh. In recognition of Theodore M. Hesburgh's "outstanding and enduring contributions to civil rights, higher education, the Catholic Church, the Nation, and the global community." Approved December 9, 1999 (P.L. 106-153; 113 Stat. 1733-1734).

John Cardinal O'Connor, Archbishop of New York. In recognition of John Cardinal O'Connor's "accomplishments as a priest, a chaplain, and a humanitarian." Approved March 3, 2000 (P.L. 106-175; 114 Stat. 20-21).

Charles M. Schulz. In recognition of Charles M. Schulz's "lasting artistic contributions to the Nation and the world." Approved June 20, 2000 (P.L. 106-225; 114 Stat. 457-458).

Pope John Paul II. In recognition of Pope John Paul II's "many and enduring contributions to peace and religious understanding." Approved July 27, 2000 (P.L. 106-250; 114 Stat. 622-623).

Ronald and Nancy Reagan. In recognition of Ronald and Nancy Reagan's "service to the Nation." Approved July 27, 2000 (P.L. 106-251; 114 Stat. 624-625).

Navajo Code Talkers. In recognition of the contribution of the original 29 Navajo Marine Corps Radio Operators, known as the Navajo Code Talkers, "who distinguished themselves in performing a unique, highly successful communications operation that greatly assisted in saving countless lives and hastening the end of World War II in the Pacific." (Silver medals were awarded to each person who qualified as a Navajo Code Talker (MOS 642).) Approved December 21, 2000 (P.L. 106-554; 114 Stat. 2763A-311—2763A-312).

General Henry H. Shelton. In recognition of the performance of General Henry H. Shelton "as a military leader in coordinating the planning, strategy, and execution of the United States and NATO combat action and his invaluable contributions to the United States and to the successful return to peace in the Balkans as Chairman of the Joint Chiefs of Staff." Approved January 16, 2002 (P.L. 107-127; 115 Stat. 2405-2406).

Prime Minister Tony Blair. In recognition of the "outstanding and enduring contributions" of Prime Minister Tony Blair of the United Kingdom "to maintaining the security of all freedom- loving nations." Approved July 17, 2003 (P.L. 108-60; 117 Stat. 862).

Jackie Robinson. In recognition of Jackie Robinson's "legacy and personal achievements," and "many contributions to the nation." Approved October 29, 2003 (P.L. 108-101; 117 Stat. 1195-1197).

Dr. Dorothy Height. In recognition of Dr. Dorothy Height's contribution "as one of the preeminent social and civil rights activists of her time, particularly in the struggle for equality, social justice, and human rights for all people." Approved December 6, 2003 (P.L. 108-162; 117 Stat. 2017-2019).

Reverend Joseph DeLaine, Harry and Eliza Briggs, and Levi Pearson. In recognition of the contributions of Reverend Joseph A. DeLaine, Harry and Eliza Briggs, and Levi Pearson "to the Nation as pioneers in the effort to desegregate public schools that led directly to the landmark desegregation case of Brown et al. v. the Board of Education of Topeka et al." Approved December 15, 2003 (P.L. 108-180; 117 Stat. 2645-2647).

Reverend Doctor Martin Luther King, Jr. and Coretta Scott King. In recognition of the contributions of Reverend Doctor Martin Luther King, Jr. and Coretta Scott King "to the Nation on behalf of the civil rights movement." Approved October 25, 2004 (P.L. 108-368; 118 Stat. 1746-1748).

Tuskegee Airmen. In recognition of the "unique military record" of the Tuskegee Airman, "which inspired revolutionary reform in the Armed Forces." Approved April 11, 2006 (P.L. 109- 213; 120 Stat. 322-325).

Gyatso, Tenzin, the Fourteenth Dalai Lama. In recognition of the "many enduring and outstanding contributions of Tenzin Gyatso, the Fourteenth Dalai Lama, "to peace, non-violence, human rights, and religious understanding." Approved September 27, 2006 (P.L. 109-287; 120 Stat. 1231-1232).

Byron Nelson. In recognition of Byron Nelson's "significant contributions to the game of golf as a player, a teacher, and a commentator." Approved October 16, 2006 (P.L. 109-357; 120 Stat. 2044-2046).

Dr. Norman E. Borlaug. In recognition of Dr. Norman E. Borlaug's "enduring contribution to the United States and the World." Approved December 14, 2006 (P.L. 109-395; 120 Stat. 2708-2710).

Dr. Michael Ellis DeBakey. In recognition of Dr. Michael Ellis DeBakey's "many outstanding contributions to the Nation." Approved October 16, 2007 (P.L. 110-95; 121 Stat. 1008-1010).

Daw Aung San Suu Kyi. In recognition of Daw Aung San Suu Kyi's "courageous and unwavering commitment to peace, nonviolence, human rights and democracy in Burma." Approved May 6, 2008 (P.L. 110-209; 122 Stat. 721-722).

Constantino Brumidi. In recognition of his contributions to the nation as a designer and decorator of the U.S. Capitol. Approved July 1, 2008 (P.L. 110-259; 122 Stat. 2430-2432).

Edward William Brooke, III. In "recognition of his unprecedented and enduring service to our Nation." Approved July 1, 2008 (P.L. 110-260; 122 Stat. 2433-2435).

Code Talkers Recognition Act of 2008. In recognition of the service of all Native American code talkers during World War I and World War II. Approved October 15, 2008 (P.L. 110-420; 122 Stat. 4774-4777).

Women Airforce Service Pilots ("WASP"). In recognition of the "pioneering military service and exemplary record" of the Women Airforce Service Pilots ("WASP"), "which forged revolutionary reform in the Armed Forces of the United States of America." Approved July 2, 2009 (P.L. 111-40; 123 Stat. 1958-1961).

Neil A. Armstrong, Edwin E. "Buzz" Aldrin, Jr., Michael Collins, and John Herschel Glenn, Jr. In recognition of the "significant contributions to society" of Neil A. Armstrong, the first human to walk on the Moon; Edwin E. "Buzz" Aldrin, Jr., the pilot of the lunar module and second person to walk on the Moon; Michael Collins, the pilot of their Apollo 11 mission's command module; and John Herschel Glenn, Jr., the first American to orbit the Earth. Approved August 7, 2009 (P.L. 111-44; 123 Stat. 1966-1967).

Arnold Palmer. In recognition of Arnold Palmer's "service to the Nation in promoting excellence and good sportsmanship in golf." Approved September 30, 2009 (P.L. 111-65; 123 Stat. 2003-2005).

Dr. Muhammad Yunus. In recognition of Dr. Yunus's "contributions to the fight against global poverty." Approved October 5, 2010 (P.L. 111-253; 124 Stat. 2635).

110th Infantry Battalion and the 442nd Regimental Combat Team, United States Army. In recognition of their "bravery, valor, and dedication to country ... while fighting a 2-fronted battle of discrimination at home and fascism abroad." Approved October 5, 2010 (P.L. 111-254; 124 Stat. 2637).

The Montford Point Marines. In recognition of "their personal sacrifice and service to their country" as the first African-American Marines. Approved November 23, 2011 (P.L. 112-59; 125 Stat. 749).

Fallen Heroes of 9/11. In "honor of the men and women who perished as a result of the terrorist attacks on the United States on September 11, 2001. Approved December 23, 2011 (P.L. 112-76;125 Stat. 1275).

Raoul Wallenberg. In "recognition of his achievements and heroic actions during the Holocaust." Approved July 26, 2012 (P.L. 112-148; 126 Stat. 1140).

End Notes

[1] See "Decorations, Medals, and Badges," in the general index of the *United States Code: 2000 Edition* (Washington: GPO, 2001).

[2] J.F. Loubat, *The Medallic History of the United States of America, 1776-1876*, 2 vols. (New York: Printed by Author, 1878), vol. 1, p. viii.

[3] Julian P. Boyd, L. H. Butterfield, Charles Cullen, and John Catanzariti, eds., *The Papers of Thomas Jefferson*, 31 vols. to date (Princeton, NJ: Princeton University Press, 1950-), vol. 16, p. 53.

[4] David Humphrey to Matthew Carey (Printer of the American Museum), November 1787, in Labatt, *The Medallic History of the United States*, vol. 1, p. xxiv.

[5] Humphrey "succeeded in securing the cooperation of the *Academe d'Insciptions et Belles-Lettres* in Paris and this learned institution nominated a committee of four among its members who worked very expeditiously in devising designs and inscriptions" for the medals the Continental Congress had authorized. Vladimir Clain-Stefanelli and Elvira Clain-Stefanelli, *Medals Commemorating Battles of the American Revolution* (Washington: The National Museum of History and Technology, Smithsonian Institution, 1973), p. 1.

[6] T. Bailey Meyers, "Our National Medals," *Magazine of American History*, vol. 2, September 1878, pp. 529-532. Altogether Congress authorized a total of 15 medals and 10 ceremonial swords during the Confederation period. Boyd, *The Papers of Thomas Jefferson*, vol. 16, pp. 54-55.

[7] U.S. Continental Congress, *Journals of the Continental Congress: 1774-1789*, vol. 4, March 25, 1776, p. 234. Brief histories of George Washington's gold medal are found in Georgia Stamm Chamberlain, *American Medals and Medalists* (Annandale, VA: Designed and Lithographed by the Turnpike Press, Inc., 1963), pp. 16-17; R.W. Julian, *Medals of the United States Mint: The First Century 1792-1892* (El Cajon, CA: The Token and Medal Society, Inc., 1977), pp. 114-115.

[8] *Journals of the Continental Congress*, vol. 9, November 4, 1777, pp. 861-862; vol. 14, July 26, 1779, p. 890.

[9] Ibid., vol. 15, September 24, 1779, p. 1099; vol. 19, January 17, 1781, pp. 246-247; vol. 21, October 19, 1781, pp. 1083-1085; vol. 33, October 16, 1787, p. 687. For discussions of these medals, see Theodore T. Belote, "War Medals of the American Revolution," *Daughters of the American Revolution Magazine*, vol. 55, September 1921, pp. 487-499; Boyd, *The Papers of Thomas Jefferson*, vol. 16, pp. xxxv-xli, 53-66; Julian, *Medals of the United States Mint*, pp. 114- 117, 120, 122, 149; Labatt, *The Medallic History of the United States*, vol. 1, pp. 1-21, 29-36, 40-45, 50-56, 97-112; Martha L. Turner, "Commemorative Medals of the American Revolution and the War of 1812," *Numismatist*, vol. 88, January 1975, pp. 6-15.

[10] Boyd, *The Papers of Thomas Jefferson*, vol. 16, pp. xxxv, 66, 288-289n; and John C. Fitzpatrick, ed., *The Writings of George Washington*, 39 vols. (Washington: GPO, 1931-1944), vol. 31, p. 27n.

[11] Julian, *Medals of the United States Mint*, p. xviii.

[12] 2 Stat. 87, 346-347. See also Theodore T. Belote, "Naval War Medals of the United States 1800-1815, Part III," *Daughters of the American Revolution Magazine*, vol. 56, January 1922, pp. 77-93; Julian, *Medals of the United States Mint*, p. 150; Labatt, *The Medallic History of the United States*, vol. 1, pp. 128-132.

[13] Theodore T. Belote, "Military and Naval Medals of the War of 1812-1815, Part II," *Daughters of the American Revolution Magazine*, vol. 55, November 1921, p. 639.

[14] 3 Stat. 341. See also Belote, "Naval War Medals of the United States 1800-1815, Part III," pp. 92-93; Julian, *Medals of the United States Mint*, p. 153; Labatt, *The Medallic History of the United States*, vol. 1, pp. 249-252.

[15] 9 Stat. 111, 206, 334-335. See also Chamberlain, *American Medals and Medalists*, pp. 75-93.

[16] 9 Stat. 333. See also Theodore T. Belote, "Military Medals of the War with Mexico and the Civil War," *Numismatist*, vol. 56, May 1922, pp. 280-281; Julian, *Medals of the United States Mint*, p. 138.

[17] 9 Stat. 208.

[18] 10 Stat. 594-595.

[19] 11 Stat. 369. See also Labatt, *The Medallic History of the United States*, vol. 2, pp. 362-369.

[20] 13 Stat. 401-402. See also U.S. President, 1861-1865 (Lincoln), Message of the President of the United States Recommending That Some Suitable Acknowledgment Be Made to Cornelius Vanderbilt for the Valuable Present to the United States of the Steamer "Vanderbilt," S. Ex. Doc. 71, 37th Cong., 2nd sess. (Washington: GPO, 1862), p. 1.

[21] 14 Stat. 574. See also U.S. President, 1865-1869 (A. Johnson), Gold Medal Presented to Cyrus W. Field. Message From the President in Relation to the Gold Medal Presented to Mr. Cyrus W. Field, H. Ex. Doc. 89, 40th Cong., 3rd sess. (Washington: GPO, 1869).

[22] 16 Stat. 704. See also U.S. Congress, House Committee on Foreign Affairs, *George F. Robinson*, report to accompany H.Res. 501, 41st Cong., 3rd sess., H.Rept. 33 (Washington: GPO, 1874).

[23] 12 Stat. 330, 623-624. See also CRS Report 95-519, *Medal of Honor: History and Issues*, by David F. Burrelli; *Above and Beyond: A History of the Medal of Honor From the Civil War to Vietnam* (Boston: Boston Publishing Co., 1985); E. Kerrigan, *American War Medals and Decorations* (New York: The Viking Press), 1964, pp. 3-11; George Lang, *Medal of Honor Recipients, 1863-1994*, 2 vols. (New York: Facts on File, 1995); U.S. Congress, Senate Committee on Veterans' Affairs, *Medal of Honor Recipients 1863-1978*, committee print

no. 3, 96th Cong., 1st sess. (Washington: GPO, 1979); Mendel L. Peterson, "The Navy Medal of Honor," *Numismatist*, vol. 63, June 1950, pp. 305-312; Ibid., "The Army Medal of Honor," *Numismatist*, vol. 63, September 1950, pp. 557 565.

24 13 Stat. 399. See also Belote, "Military Medals of the War with Mexico and the Civil War," p. 282; Julian, *Medals of the United States Mint*, p. 140.

25 14 Stat. 365-366; and 17 Stat. 638. See also U.S. Congress, House Committee on Commerce, *Steamship San Francisco*, H.Rept. 97, 39th Cong., 1st sess. (Washington: GPO, 1866); Julian, *Medals of the United States Mint*, pp. 328, 332; Labatt, *The Medallic History of the United States*, vol. 2, pp. 412-417.

26 18 Stat. 573. A lengthy account of Horn's heroics is found in "John Horn, Jr., of Detroit: The Man to Whom Congress Voted a Gold Medal for His Exertions in Saving Life," *New York Times*, June 28, 1874, p. 9. On April 28, 1904, Congress authorized and directed the Secretary of the Treasury to strike and present to John Horn, Jr., a duplicate of the medal voted by Congress to him in 1874, which had been stolen from him in October 1901. 33 Stat. 1684-1685. See also Julian, *Medals of the United States Mint*, p. 331.

27 25 Stat. 1249. See also U.S. Congress, House Committee on Commerce, *Joseph Francis*, H.Rept. 529, 49th Cong., 1st sess. (Washington: GPO, 1886).

28 26 Stat. 552-553. See also U.S. Congress, House Committee on Naval Affairs, *Officers and Men of the Jeannette Arctic Expedition*, H.Rept. 3183, 51st Cong., 1st sess. (Washington: GPO, 1891).

29 15 Stat. 20; 22 Stat. 636. See also U.S. President, 1865-1869 (A. Johnson), Gold Medal to George Peabody: Message From the President of the United States in Relation to the Gold Medal Presented to George Peabody, H. Exec. Doc. 53, 40th Cong., 3rd sess. (Washington: GPO, 1869); U.S. Congress, Senate Committee on Education and Labor, In the Senate of the United States (Report on John F. Slater), H.Rept. 935, 47th Cong., 2nd sess. (Washington: GPO, 1883); U.S. Congress, Joint Committee on the Library, John F. Slater, H.Rept. 869, 49th Cong., 1st sess. (Washington: GPO, 1886).

30 49 Stat. 2371; 68 Stat. A120. See also U.S. Congress, House Committee on the Library, *To Authorize the President to Present a Gold Medal to George M. Cohan in Recognition of His Patriotic Service*, H.Rept. 2868, 74th Cong., 2nd sess. (Washington: GPO, 1936); and U.S. Congress, House Committee on Banking and Currency, *The Irving Berlin Medal*, H.Rept. 1999, 83rd Cong., 2nd sess. (Washington: GPO, 1954).

31 74 Stat. 883; 76 Stat. 93; and 82 Stat. 130-131. See also U.S. Congress, Senate Committee on Banking and Currency, *Robert Frost Medal*, S.Rept. 1572, 86th Cong., 2nd sess. (Washington: GPO, 1960); U.S. Congress, House Committee on Banking and Currency, *Authorizing the Issuance of a Gold Medal to Bob Hope*, H.Rept. 1716, 87th Cong., 2nd sess. (Washington: GPO, 1962); Ibid., *Walt Disney Commemorative Medals*, H.Rept. 1342, 90th Cong., 2nd sess. (Washington: GPO, 1968).

32 91 Stat. 19; 93 Stat. 32. See also U.S. Congress, Senate Committee on Banking, Housing, and Urban Affairs, *Authorizing the Issuance of a Gold Medal to John Wayne*. S.Rept. 96-110, 96th Cong., 1st sess. (Washington: GPO, 1979).

33 96 Stat. 315-316; 97 Stat. 1119-1120; 98 Stat. 173-175. See also U.S. Congress, House Committee on Banking, Finance and Urban Affairs, Subcommittee on Consumer Affairs and Coinage, *Gold Medal for Fred Waring*, hearings on H.J.Res. 223, 97th Cong., 1st sess., July 22, 1981 (Washington: GPO, 1981); Ibid., *To Present a Gold Medal to Danny Thomas*, hearings on H.J.Res. 93, 98th Cong., 1st sess., October 18, 1983 (Washington: GPO, 1983); "Authorizing Awarding of Special Congressional Gold Medals to Daughter of Harry S. Truman, Lady Bird Johnson, and Elie Wiesel," *Congressional Record*, vol. 130 (April 26, 1984), pp. 10223-10225.

34 100 Stat 464. See also U.S. Congress, House Committee on Banking, Finance and Urban Affairs, Subcommittee on Consumer Affairs and Coinage, *To Provide Gold Medals Honoring the Family of Harry Chapin; Anatoly and Avital Shcharansky*, hearings on H.R. 1207 and H.R. 4186, 99th Cong., 2nd sess., May 1, 1986 (Washington: GPO, 1986).

[35] 99 Stat. 288-289; 100 Stat. 952; 102 Stat. 3331-3332; 111 Stat. 32-33; 114 Stat. 457-458. See also U.S. Congress, House Committee on Banking, Finance, and Urban Affairs, Subcommittee on Consumer Affairs and Coinage, *To Provide Special Gold Medals Honoring George and Ira Gershwin*, hearings on H.J.Res. 251, 99th Cong., 1st sess., July 10, 1985 (Washington: GPO, 1985); Ibid., *To Award a Special Congressional Gold Medal to Aaron Copland*, hearings on H.R. 3041, 99th Cong., 2nd sess., August 6, 1986 (Washington: GPO, 1986); Ibid., *Gold Medal for Jesse Owens*—H.R. 1270, *Gold Medal for Andrew Wyeth*—H.R. 593, hearings, 100th Cong., 2nd sess., July 12, 1988 (Washington: GPO, 1988), pp. 15-19, 39-47.

[36] 122 Stat. 2430-2432.

[37] 35 Stat. 1627. See also "Gold Medal by Congress to Wright Brothers," *Numismatist*, vol. 22, August 1919, pp. 231- 232; Arthur L. Newman, "Some Medals Struck in Honor of the Wright Brothers," *Numismatist*, vol. 81, December 1968, p. 1576.

[38] 45 Stat. 490. See also U.S. Congress, House Committee on Coinage, Weights, and Measures, *Authorizing the Coinage of a Gold Medal in Commemoration of the Achievements of Col. Charles A. Lindbergh*, H.Rept. 722, 70th Cong., 1st sess. (Washington: GPO, 1928).

[39] 45 Stat. 1158; 53 Stat. 152; 60 Stat. 1319. See also U.S. Congress, House Committee on Naval Affairs, *To Authorize the President to Award, in the Name of Congress, Gold Medals of Appropriate Design to Albert C. Read, Elmer F. Stone, Walter Hinton, H.C. Rodd, J. L. Breese, and Eugene Rhodes*, H.Rept. 2082, 70th Cong., 2nd sess. (Washington: GPO, 1929); U.S. Congress, House Committee on Coinage, Weights, and Measures, *Howard Hughes*, H.Rept. 1339, 76th Cong., 1st sess. (Washington: GPO, 1939); U.S. Congress, House Committee on Military Affairs, *Authorizing the Award of a Medal to William Mitchell*, H.Rept. 2625, 79th Cong., 2nd sess. (Washington: GPO, 1946).

[40] 73 Stat. 562-563; 92 Stat. 1060; 93 Stat. 45. See also U.S. Congress, House Committee on Banking and Currency, *Gold Medal Honoring the Late Prof. Robert H. Goddard*, H.Rept. 882, 86th Cong., 1st sess. (Washington: GPO, 1959); Ibid., *Presentation of Gold Medal to Lt. Gen. Ira C. Eaker*, H.Rept. 95-1603, 95th Cong., 2nd sess. (Washington: GPO, 1978); and U.S. Congress, Senate Committee on Banking, Housing and Urban Affairs, *Authorizing the Issuance of Gold Medals to the First Transatlantic Balloonists: Ben Abruzzo, Maxie Anderson, and Larry Newman*, H.J.Res. 223. 96-108, 96th Cong., 1st sess. (Washington: GPO, 1979).

[41] 123 Stat. 1966-1967.

[42] 45 Stat. 2026-2027. See also U.S. Congress, Senate Committee on Commerce, *A Medal of Honor to Lincoln Ellsworth*, S.Rept. 831, 70th Cong., 1st sess. (Washington: GPO, 1928).

[43] 46 Stat. 379; and 49 Stat. 2324. See also U.S. Congress, Senate Committee on Naval Affairs. *Authorizing the Presentation of Medals to the Officers and Men of the Byrd Antarctic Expedition*, S.Rept. 688, 71st Cong., 2nd sess. (Washington: GPO, 1930); U.S. Congress, House Committee on Coinage, Weights, and Measures, *Proposing the Presentation of Medals to the Officers and Men of the Byrd Antarctic Expedition*, H.Rept. 1402, 71st Cong., 2nd sess. (Washington: GPO, 1930); U.S. Congress, Senate Committee on Commerce, *Special Gold Medal to Lincoln Ellsworth*, S.Rept. 1658, 74th Cong., 2nd sess. (Washington: GPO, 1936).

[44] For example see 18 Stat. 127; 33 Stat. 743; 71 Stat. 69.

[45] 16 Stat. 704.

[46] 14 Stat. 365-366; and 17 Stat. 638. See also U.S. Congress, House Committee on Commerce, *Steamship San Francisco*, H.Rept. 97, 39th Cong., 1st sess. (Washington: GPO, 1866); Julian, *Medals of the United States Mint*, pp. 328, 332; Labatt, *The Medallic History of the United States*, vol. 2, pp. 412-417. See also Edouard A. Stackpole, comp., *The Wreck of the Steamer San Francisco* (Mystic, CT: The Maine Historical Society Association, Inc., December 1954).

[47] 17 Stat. 638.

[48] 18 Stat. 573.

[49] 25 Stat. 1249.

[50] 32 Stat. 492; 37 Stat, 639; and 38 Stat. 769. See also U.S. Congress, House Committee on Interstate and Foreign Commerce, *Medals to Certain Officers in the Revenue Service*, H.Rept. 2336, 57th Cong., 1st sess. (Washington: GPO, 1902); U.S. Congress, House Committee on Merchant Marines and Fisheries, *Capt. Arthur Henry Rostron*, H.Rept. 830, 62nd Cong., 2nd sess. (Washington: GPO, 1912).

[51] 53 Stat. 1533; 54 Stat. 1283; and 56 Stat 1099-1100. See also U.S. Congress, House Committee on Coinage, Weights, and Measures, *Rev. Francis X. Quinn*, H.Rept. 1338, 76th Cong. 1st sess. (Washington: GPO, 1939); U.S. Congress, House Committee on the Library, *Presentation of a Medal (Roland Boucher)*, H.Rept. 431, 77th Cong., 1st sess. (Washington: GPO, 1941).

[52] 31 Stat. 716. See also U.S. Congress, House Committee on Interstate and Foreign Commerce, *Lieut. Frank H. Newcomb, Etc.*, H.Rept. 302, 56th Cong., 1st sess. (Washington: GPO, 1900); U.S. Congress, Senate Committee on Commerce, *Lieut. Frank H. Newcomb, Etc.*, S.Rept. 29, 56th Cong., 1st sess. (Washington: GPO, 1900).

[53] 60 Stat. 1134; and 1297. See also U.S. Congress, Senate Committee on Military Affairs, *Tendering the Thanks of Congress to General of the Army George Catlett Marshall and to Fleet Admiral Ernest Joseph King*, S.Rept. 983, 79th Cong., 2nd sess. (Washington: GPO, 1946); Ibid., *Medal for General Pershing*, S.Rept. 1832, 79th Cong., 2nd sess. (Washington: GPO, 1946).

[54] 70 Stat. 577. See also U.S. Congress, Senate Committee on Banking and Currency, *Civil War Veterans Medals*, S.Rept. 2423, 84th Cong., 2nd sess. (Washington: GPO, 1956).

[55] 72 Stat. 985; 96 Stat. 126-127. See also "Conferring of Medal on Rear Adm. Hyman George Rickover, United States Navy," *Congressional Record*, vol. 104, August 18, 1958, pp. 18107-18108; "Rear Adm. Hyman George Rickover," *Congressional Record*, vol. 4, August 18, 1958, pp. 18345-18355; U.S. Congress, House Committee on Banking, Finance, and Urban Affairs, Subcommittee on Consumer Affairs and Coinage, *Gold Medal for Admiral Hyman George Rickover*, hearing on H.R. 5432, 97th Cong., 2nd sess. (Washington: GPO, 1982).

[56] 76 Stat. 760. See also U.S. Congress, Senate Committee on Banking and Currency, *General of the Army Douglas MacArthur Medal*, S.Rept. 2116, 87th Cong., 2nd sess. (Washington: GPO, 1963).

[57] P.L. 101-510, 104 Stat. 1720-1721; P.L. 102-32, 104 Stat. 175-176; P.L. 102-33, 104 Stat. 177-178.

[58] P.L. 106-554; 114 Stat. 2763A-311—2763A-312.

[59] P.L. 110-420; 122 Stat. 4774-4777. See also: "Code Talkers Recognition Act of 2008," *Congressional Record*, daily edition, v. 153 (September 23, 2008), pp. H8696-H8699.

[60] P.L. 107-127; 115 Stat. 2405-2406.

[61] 120 Stat. 322-325. See also Rep. Charles B. Rangel, "The Tuskegee Airmen—A Hero's Welcome," Congressional Record, daily edition, vol. 150 (July 13, 2005), p. E1484-E1485; and "Authorizing the President to Award a Congressional Gold Medal to the Tuskegee Airmen," *Congressional Record*, daily edition, vol. 151 (February 28, 2006), pp. H407-H414. Authorizing legislation, H.R. 1259, 109th Cong., became P.L. 109-213 on April 11, 2006. U.S. President (George W. Bush), "Remarks on Presenting the Congressional Gold Medal to the Tuskegee Airmen, March 29, 2007," *Weekly Compilation of Presidential Documents*, vol. 43, no. 13, April 2, 2007, pp. 387-388 http://frwebgate. access&docid=pd02ap07_txt- 15.pdf. Information on distribution of the bronze duplicates was provided by Ron Brewington, Public Relations Officer, Tuskegee Airmen, Inc., May 2, 2007 (323-533-1036).

[62] P.L. 111-40; 123 Stat. 1958-1961

[63] 124 Stat. 2637.

[64] P.L. 112-59; 125 Stat. 749.

[65] P.L. 112-76.

[66] 45 Stat. 1409-1410; 52 Stat. 1365. See also U.S. Congress, Senate Committee on Military Affairs, *To Recognize the High Public Service Rendered by Major Walter Reed and Those Associated with Him in the Discovery of the Cause and Means of Transmission of Yellow Fever*, S.Rept. 1912, 70th Cong., 2nd sess. (Washington: GPO, 1929); Ibid., *Authorizing the President to Present Gold Medals to Mrs. Robert Aldrich and Posthumously to Anna Bouligny*, S.Rept. 1745, 75th Cong., 3rd sess. (Washington: GPO, 1938).

[67] 45 Stat. 1012; 69 Stat. 589; 75 Stat. 87; 101 Stat. 1441; P.L. 109-395; 120 stat. 2708-2710; P.L. 110-95; 121 Stat. 1008-1010. See also U.S. Congress, Senate Committee on Coinage, Weights, and Measures, *Authorizing a Gold Medal in Commemoration of the Achievements of Thomas A. Edison*, S.Rept. 1285, 70th Cong., 1st sess. (Washington: GPO, 1928); U.S. Congress, House Committee on Banking and Currency, Medal for *Dr. Jonas E. Salk*, H.Rept. 1351, 84th Cong., 1st sess. (Washington: GPO, 1955); U.S. Congress, Senate Committee on Banking and Currency, *Medal for Dr. Thomas Anthony Dooley III*, S.Rept. 257, 87th Cong., 1st sess. (Washington: GPO, 1961); U.S. Congress, House Committee on Banking, Finance, and Urban Affairs, Subcommittee on Consumer Affairs and Coinage, *Gold Medal for Mary Lasker* (H.R. 390), hearings on H.R. 390, 100th Cong., 1st sess., September 15, 1987 (Washington: GPO, 1987).

[68] 63 Stat. 599; See also U.S. Congress, Senate Committee on Banking and Currency, *Medal for Vice President Alben W. Barkley*, S.Rept. 742, 81st Cong., 1st sess. (Washington: GPO, 1949).

[69] 76 Stat. 605; 92 Stat. 2142; 93 Stat. 46; 97 Stat. 992; 98 Stat. 173-175; 112 Stat. 2681-598; 114 Stat. 624-625. See also U.S. Congress, Senate Committee on Banking and Currency, *Sam Rayburn Medal*, S.Rept. 2021, 87th Cong., 2nd sess. (Washington: GPO, 1962); Ibid., *Authorizing the President of the United States to Present a Gold Medal to the Widow of Robert F. Kennedy*, S.Rept. 95-1316, 95th Cong., 2nd sess. (Washington: GPO, 1978); Ibid., *Authorizing the Issuance of a Gold Medal to the Widow of Hubert H. Humphrey*, S.Rept. 96-109, 96th Cong., 1st sess. (Washington: GPO, 1979); U.S. Congress, House Committee on Banking, Finance, and Urban Affairs, Subcommittee on Consumer Affairs and Coinage, *Gold Medals to the Daughter of Harry S. Truman; Lady Bird Johnson; and the Widow of Roy Wilkins*, hearings on H.R. 3614, H.J.Res. 394, and H.R. 3240, 98th Cong., 2nd sess., March 6, 1984 (Washington: GPO, 1984); U.S. Congress, Senate Committee on Banking, Housing, and Urban Affairs, *Awarding a Congressional Gold Medal to Former President Ronald Reagan and Former First Lady Nancy Reagan: Report to Accompany S. 2459*, S.Rept. 106-357, 106th Cong., 2nd sess. (Washington: GPO, 2000); U.S. Congress, House Committee on Banking, Finance, and Urban Affairs, Subcommittee on Consumer Affairs and Coinage, *To Present a Gold Medal to the Family of the Late Honorable Leo J. Ryan ...*, hearings on H.R. 3348 and H.R. 3321, 98th Cong., 1st sess., September 20, 1983 (Washington: GPO, 1983).

[70] 122 Stat. 2433-2435.

[71] 87 Stat. 71; 96 Stat. 315; 102 Stat. 1717; 117 Stat. 1195-1197; 120 Stat. 2044-2046; and 123 Stat. 2003-2005. See also U.S. Congress, Senate Committee on Banking, Housing, and Urban Affairs; *Roberto Walker Clemente Medal*, S.Rept. 93-133, 93rd Cong., 1st sess. (Washington: GPO, 1973); "Gold Medal Bill," *Congressional Record*, vol. 128, August 2, 1982, pp. 18790-18793; U.S. Congress, House Committee on Banking, Finance, and Urban Affairs, Subcommittee on Consumer Affairs and Coinage, *Gold Medal for Jesse Owens*—H.R. 1270, *Gold Medal for Andrew Wyeth*—H.R. 593, hearings, 100th Cong., 2nd sess., July 12, 1988 (Washington: GPO, 1988).

[72] 98 Stat. 173-174; 112 Stat. 2681-597; 113 Stat. 50-51; 117 Stat. 2017-2019; 117 Stat. 2645-2647; 118 Stat. 1746-1748. See also *Gold Medals to the Daughter of Harry S. Truman; Lady Bird Johnson; and the Widow of Roy Wilkins*, pp. 11-108.

[73] 98 Stat. 173-174, 186; 104 Stat. 197-199. See also *Gold Medals to the Daughter of Harry S. Truman; Lady Bird Johnson; and the Widow of Roy Wilkins*, pp. 11-108.

[74] 108 Stat. 4799-4800; 110 Stat. 772-777.

[75] 112 Stat. 2681-598.
[76] 111 Stat. 35-36, 1170-1171; 112 Stat. 895-896.
[77] 113 Stat. 1733-1734; 114 Stat. 20-21; 114 Stat. 622-633.
[78] 120 Stat. 1231-1232; 122 Stat. 721-722.
[79] 124 Stat. 2635.
[80] 93 Stat. 1063. See also U.S. Congress, Senate Committee on Banking, Housing, and Urban Affairs, *Authorizing the Issuance of a Gold Medal to the American Red Cross*, S.Rept. 96-429, 96th Cong., 1st sess. (Washington: GPO, 1979).
[81] 9 Stat. 208.
[82] 11 Stat. 369. See also Labatt, *The Medallic History of the United States*, vol. 2, pp. 362-369.
[83] 14 Stat. 365-366; and 17 Stat. 638. See also U.S. Congress, House Committee on Commerce, *Steamship San Francisco*, H.Rept. 97, 39th Cong., 1st sess. (Washington: GPO, 1866); Julian, *Medals of the United States Mint*, pp. 328, 332; Labatt, *The Medallic History of the United States*, vol. 2, pp. 412-417. See also Edouard A. Stackpole, comp., *The Wreck of the Steamer San Francisco* (Mystic, CT: The Maine Historical Society Association, Inc., December 1954).
[84] 38 Stat. 1228.
[85] 45 Stat. 2026-2027. See also U.S. Congress, Senate Committee on Commerce, *A Medal of Honor to Lincoln Ellsworth*, S.Rept. 831, 70th Cong., 1st sess. (Washington: GPO, 1928).
[86] 83 Stat. 8-9. See also U.S. Congress, Senate Committee on Banking and Currency, *The Winston Churchill Medal*, S.Rept. 91-95, 91st Cong., 1st sess. (Washington: GPO, 1969).
[87] 94 Stat. 79. See also U.S. Congress, House Committee on Banking, Finance, and Urban Affairs, Subcommittee on Consumer Affairs and Coinage, *Legislation Authorizing Issuance of Gold Medals to Canadian Ambassador Kenneth Taylor; Simon Wiesenthal; Gerald F. Spiess; Commemorative Medals for the United States Capitol Historical Society*, hearings, 96th Cong., 2nd sess., February 8, 1980 (Washington: GPO, 1980), pp. 1-3, 11-39.
[88] 94 Stat. 101. See also U.S. Congress, Senate Committee on Banking, Housing, and Urban Affairs, *Authorizing the Issuance of a Gold Medal to Simon Wiesenthal*, S.Rept. 96-435, 96th Cong., 1st sess. (Washington: GPO, 1980).
[89] 96 Stat. 18-19. See also "Gold Medal for Queen Beatrix," *Congressional Record*, vol. 128, March 2, 1982, pp. 2730- 2732; and "Senate Joint Resolution 157—Awarding of a Special Gold Medal to Her Majesty Queen Beatrix," *Congressional Record*, vol. 128 (March 4, 1982), pp. 3280-3281.
[90] 100 Stat. 432-433. See also *To Provide Gold Medals Honoring the Family of Harry Chapin; Anatoly and Avital Shcharansky*, pp. 45-62.
[91] 111 Stat. 35-36, 1170-1171; 112 Stat. 895-896.
[92] 114 Stat. 622-623.
[93] 117 Stat. 862.
[94] 120 Stat. 1231-1232.
[95] 122 Stat. 721-722; 124 Stat. 2635.
[96] 126 Stat. 1140.
[97] An executive order (E.O. 3524) signed by President Warren G. Harding on July 28, 1921, provided "that essential matters relating to the design of medals, insignia and coins, produced by the executive departments ... shall be submitted to the Commission of Fine Arts for advice as to the merits of such designs" before the Secretary of the Treasury approves them. For current language, see 45 C.F.R. 2101.1(d), and 2102.11.
[98] Presidents do not, however, always make the presentations. Vice President George H. W. Bush presented the Red Cross Gold Medal to board chairman Jerome H. Holland at Constitution Hall in Washington on May 21, 1981. "Personalities," *Washington Post*, May 22, 1981, p. F2. Sen. Strom Thurmond presented Admiral Hyman J. Rickover's second gold medal to Mr. Rickover in the Capitol's Statuary Hall on November 1, 1983. Elizabeth Kastor, "Medal for Military Maverick," *Washington Post*, November 2, 1983, pp. B1, B8. Sen. Patrick J. Leahy presented the Harry Chapin Gold Medal to Chapin's widow at Carnegie

Hall in New York on December 7, 1987. Barbara Jaefer, "Tribute to a Benevolent Voice," *Bergen Record*, December 8, 1987, p. C1. Rep. José Serrano presented the Frank Sinatra Gold Medal to Sinatra's daughter Nancy Sinatra in his Capitol Hill office on June 5, 1998. Richard Sisk, "Congress Hails Frank," *New York Daily News*, June 6, 1998, p. 8.

[99] 31 U.S.C. 5134 (b).

[100] See for example P.L. 105-51, 114 Stat. 624-625.

[101] Congressional Gold Medals generally are three inches in diameter and contain approximately 15 ounces of gold, depending on the height of the design relief. During the Administration of President Jimmy Carter, when gold was quite expensive, the size and the weight of the medals were reduced to 1½ inches in diameter and contained 1½ to two ounces of gold. Subsequently, when the price of gold dropped after President Ronald Reagan took office, the former dimension and weight were restored. Three inch bronze duplicates and 1½ inch bronze replicas of the each medal are sold by the Mint to help recover the cost of striking a gold medal. Manufacturing and material costs dictate the price of the reproductions.

[102] "Publication of Committee Rules," *Congressional Record*, daily edition, vol. 159 (February 15, 2013), p. H578.

[103] "Committee on Banking, Housing, and Urban Affairs Rules of Procedure," *Congressional Record*, daily edition, vol. 159 (February 26, 2013), pp. S859.

[104] See "Decorations, Medals, and Badges," in the general index of the *United States Code: 2000 Edition* (Washington: GPO, 2001).

[105] Rule 28(a)(7), *Rules of the House Republican Conference for the 113th Congress*, available at http://www.gop.gov/ about/rules?rules-home.

[106] The elected leadership of the Republican Conference is defined in Rule 2(a) of the Conference Rules to include the Speaker of the House, the Republican Leader, the Republican Whip, the Chair of the Republican Conference, the Chairman of the National Republican Congressional Committee, the Chair of the Committee on Policy, the Vice- Chairman of the Republican Conference, and the Secretary of the Republican Conference.

[107] "Congressional Gold Medal Enhancement Act of 2005," *Congressional Record*, daily edition, vol. 151 (January 26, 2004), pp. H207. See also "Limits May Be Imposed on Honor Medals," *Washington Post*, January 27, 2005, p. A17.

[108] "Congressional Gold Medal Enhancement Act of 2005," *Congressional Record*, daily edition, vol. 151 (January 26, 2004), pp. H206.

[109] Ibid., pp. H206-H207, H209.

[110] Ibid., pp. H211, H213, H215-H216.

In: Congressional Gold Medals: 1776-2013 ISBN: 978-1-62948-848-6
Editor: Amanda Perry-Jenkins © 2014 Nova Science Publishers, Inc.

Chapter 2

Public Law 113–11 113th Congress (Congressional Gold Medal Posthumously Awarded to Addie Mae Collins, Denise McNair, Carole Robertson, and Cynthia Wesley)*

An Act

McNair, Carole Robertson, and Cynthia Wesley to commemorate the lives they lost 50 years ago in the bombing of the Sixteenth Street Baptist Church, where these 4 little Black girls' ultimate sacrifice served as a catalyst for the Civil Rights Movement.

Be it enacted by the Senate and House of Representatives of the United States of America in Congress assembled,

Section 1. Findings

The Congress Finds the following:

(1) September 15, 2013, will mark 50 years since the lives of Addie Mae Collins, Denise McNair, Carole Robertson, and Cynthia Wesley were

* This is an edited, reformatted and augmented version of a Public Law 113–11, dated May 24, 2013.

suddenly taken by a bomb planted in the Sixteenth Street Baptist Church in Birmingham, Alabama.

(2) The senseless and premature death of these 4 little Black girls sparked ''The Movement that Changed the World''.

(3) On that tragic Sunday in September of 1963, the world took notice of the violence inflicted in the struggle for equal rights.

(4) The fact that 4 innocent children lost their lives as they prepared for Sunday School shook the world's conscience. (5) This tragedy galvanized the Civil Rights Movement and sparked a surge of momentum that helped secure the passage of the Civil Rights Act of 1964 and later the Voting Rights Act of 1965 by President Lyndon B. Johnson.

(6) Justice was delayed for these 4 little Black girls and their families until 2002, 39 years after the bombing, when the last of the 4 Klansmen responsible for the bombing was charged and convicted of the crime.

(7) The 4 little Black girls are emblematic of so many who have lost their lives for the cause of freedom and equality, including Virgil Ware and James Johnny Robinson who were children also killed within hours of the 1963 church bombing. (8) The legacy that these 4 little Black girls left will live on in the minds and hearts of us all for generations to come. (9) Their extraordinary sacrifice sparked real and lasting change as Congress began to aggressively pass legislation that ensured equality.

(10) Sixteenth Street Baptist Church remains a powerful symbol of the movement for civil and human rights and will host the 50th anniversary ceremony on Sunday, September 15, 2013.

(11) It is befitting that Congress bestow the highest civilian honor, the Congressional Gold Medal, in 2013 to the 4 little Black girls, Addie Mae Collins, Denise McNair, Carole Robert- son, and Cynthia Wesley, posthumously in recognition of the 50th commemoration of the historical significance of the bombing of the Sixteenth Street Baptist Church.

SEC. 2. Congressional Gold Medal

(a) PRESENTATION AUTHORIZED.—The Speaker of the House of Representatives and the President Pro Tempore of the Senate shall make appropriate arrangements for the presentation, on behalf of Congress, of a gold medal of appropriate design to commemorate the lives of Addie Mae Collins, Denise McNair, Carole Robertson, and Cynthia Wesley.

(b) DESIGN AND STRIKING.—For purposes of the presentation referred to in subsection (a), the Secretary of the Treasury (referred to in this Act as the ''Secretary'') shall strike a gold medal with suitable emblems, devices, and inscriptions to be determined by the Secretary.

(c) AWARD OF MEDAL.—Following the award of the gold medal described in subsection (a), the medal shall be given to the Bir- mingham Civil Rights Institute in Birmingham, AL, where it shall be available for display or temporary loan to be displayed elsewhere, as appropriate.

Sec. 3. Duplicate Medals

The Secretary may strike and sell duplicates in bronze of the gold medal struck under section 2, at a price sufficient to cover the costs of the medal, including labor, materials, dies, use of machinery, and overhead expenses, and amounts received from the sale of such duplicates shall be deposited in the United States Mint Public Enterprise Fund.

Sec. 4. Status of Medals

(a) NATIONAL MEDALS.—The medals struck under this Act are national medals for purposes of chapter 51 of title 31, United States Code.

(b) NUMISMATIC ITEMS.—For purposes of sections 5134 and 5136 of title 31, United States Code, all medals struck under this Act shall be considered to be numismatic items.

Approved May 24, 2013.

In: Congressional Gold Medals: 1776-2013 ISBN: 978-1-62948-848-6
Editor: Amanda Perry-Jenkins

Chapter 3

Public Law 113–16 113th Congress (Congressional Gold Medal, Collectively, to the First Special Service Force, World War II)*

An Act

To grant the Congressional Gold Medal, collectively, to the First Special Service Force, in recognition of its superior service during World War II.

Be it enacted by the Senate and House of Representatives of the United States of America in Congress assembled,

Section 1. Findings

Congress finds the following:

(1) The First Special Service Force (the ''Force''), a military unit composed of volunteers from the United States and Canada, was activated in July 1942 at Fort Harrison near Helena, Montana.

(2) The Force was initially intended to target military and industrial installations that were supporting the German war effort, including important hydroelectric plants, which would severely limit the production of strategic materials used by the Axis powers.

* This is an edited, reformatted and augmented version of a PUBLIC LAW 113–16, dated JULY 12, 2013.

(3) From July 1942 through June 1943, volunteers of the Force trained in hazardous, arctic conditions in the mountains of western Montana, and in the waterways of Camp Bradford, Virginia.

(4) The combat echelon of the Force totaled 1,800 soldiers, half from the United States and half from Canada.

(5) The Force also contained a service battalion, composed of 800 members from the United States, that provided important support for the combat troops.

(6) A special bond developed between the Canadian and United States soldiers, who were not segregated by country, although the commander of the Force was a United Statescolonel.

(7) The Force was the only unit formed during World War II that consisted of troops from Canada and the United States.

(8) In October 1943, the Force went to Italy, where it fought in battles south of Cassino, including Monte La Difensa and Monte Majo, two mountain peaks that were a critical anchor of the German defense line.

(9) During the night of December 3, 1943, the Force ascended to the top of the precipitous face of Monte La Difensa, where the Force suffered heavy casualties and overcame fierce resistance to overtake the German line.

(10) After the battle for La Difensa, the Force continued to fight tough battles at high altitudes, in rugged terrain, and in severe weather.

(11) After battles on the strongly defended Italian peaks of Sammucro, Vischiataro, and Remetanea, the size of the Force had been reduced from 1,800 soldiers to fewer than 500.

(12) For 4 months in 1944, the Force engaged in raids and aggressive patrols at the Anzio Beachhead.

(13) On June 4, 1944, members of the Force were among the first Allied troops to liberate Rome.

(14) After liberating Rome, the Force moved to southern Italy and prepared to assist in the liberation of France.

(15) During the early morning of August 15, 1944, members of the Force made silent landings on Les Iles D'Hyeres, small islands in the Mediterranean Sea along the southern coast of France.

(16) The Force faced a sustained and withering assault from the German garrisons as the Force progressed from the islands to the Franco-Italian border.

(17) After the Allied forces secured the Franco-Italian border, the United States Army ordered the disbandment of the Force on December 5, 1944, in Nice, France.

(18) During 251 days of combat, the Force suffered 2,314 casualties, or 134 percent of its authorized strength, captured thousands of prisoners, won 5 United States campaign stars and 8 Canadian battle honors, and never failed a mission.

(19) The United States is forever indebted to the acts of bravery and selflessness of the troops of the Force, who risked their lives for the cause of freedom.

(20) The efforts of the Force along the seas and skies of Europe were critical in repelling the advance of Nazi Germany and liberating numerous communities in France and Italy.

(21) The bond between the members of the Force from the United States and those from Canada has endured over the decades, as the members meet every year for a reunion, alternating between the United States and Canada.

(22) The traditions and honors exhibited by the Force are carried on by 2 outstanding active units of 2 great democracies, the Special Forces of the United States and the Canadian Special Operations Regiment.

Sec. 2. Congressional Gold Medal

(a) AWARD AUTHORIZED.—The Speaker of the House of Representatives and the President pro tempore of the Senate shall make appropriate arrangements for the award, on behalf of the Congress, of a gold medal of appropriate design to the First Special Service Force, collectively, in recognition of their dedicated service during World War II.

(b) DESIGN AND STRIKING.—For the purposes of the award referred to in subsection (a), the Secretary of the Treasury (in this Act referred to as the ''Secretary'') shall strike the gold medal with suitable emblems, devices, and inscriptions, to be determined by the Secretary.

(c) AWARD OF MEDAL.—Following the award of the gold medal in honor of the First Special Service Force under subsection (a), the medal shall be given to the First Special Service Force Associa- tion in Helena, Montana, where it shall be available for display or temporary loan to be displayed elsewhere, particularly at other appropriate locations associated with the First Special Service Force, including Fort William Henry Harrison in Helena, Montana.

Sec. 3. Duplicate Medals

The Secretary may strike and sell duplicates in bronze of the gold medal struck under section 2, at a price sufficient to cover the costs of the medal, including labor, materials, dies, use of machinery, and overhead expenses, and amounts received from the sale of such duplicates shall be deposited in the United States Mint Public Enterprise Fund.

Sec. 4. National Medals

Medals struck pursuant to this Act are national medals for purposes of chapter 51 of title 31, United States Code.

Approved July 12, 2013.

INDEX

#

A

B

C

D

E

F

G

H

I

R

S

T

U

V

W

Y